10.95

CONQUERING *the* KILL-JOYS

'This is a _must read_ book'
MARY KAY ASH

CONQUERING the KILL-JOYS

POSITIVE LIVING IN A NEGATIVE WORLD

BILL WEBER

WORD BOOKS
PUBLISHER
WACO, TEXAS

A DIVISION OF
WORD, INCORPORATED

Library of Congress Cataloging in Publication Data:

Weber, Bill, 1942–
Conquering the kill-joys.

1. Christian life—1960–   I. Title.
BV4501.2.W4146   1986   248.4   86–4024
ISBN   0–8499–0439–0

67898 BKC 987654321

Printed in the United States of America

This book is dedicated to my father,
Dr. Jaroy Weber, who through his patience,
kindness, and sincere love has enriched my
life with wisdom and understanding for the
hurts and needs of others.

CONTENTS

CONQUERING the KILL-JOYS

FOREWORD

Bill Weber has been my pastor for many years. He is one of the most sensitive men in the Christian arena today, bringing practical messages to his congregation week after week. His keen insight into the problems of our age, coupled with his ability to use the Scriptures in a dynamic way, enable him to deliver an extremely applicable message for men and women across our country. He is a man who committed his life to applying the Bible in a very practical way to soothe and heal the wounds that are festering throughout America and our entire world.

As I began reading *Conquering the Kill-Joys,* I found it hard to put down—it so candidly relates all the challenges with which we live in our society. Many workable answers flow from the pages of this book, practical answers to the pressures of our uptight and fast-paced generation. Resentment . . . discouragement . . . loneliness. . . . They are problems we all face, but Bill shows us that we don't have to live with them!

Bill's exuberant zest for finding and sharing the abundant life is evident in each chapter. His desire for this book is that it will enable you to *Conquer the Kill-Joys* and live the wonderfully exciting way that God intended. This is a *must read* book.

MARY KAY ASH

INTRODUCTION

God made each of us with the capacity for greatness and joy, but many people go through life never achieving their full potential. He intends for us to live happy, joyful lives, but so often we are too weighted down with the "kill-joys" of life to even think about being happy. This book is an attempt to share truths that I am learning in the process of dealing with life's greatest hurts. We were never promised that we would be exempt from problems, but we *were* assured that our personal faith would be adequate for whatever problems we might face.

I would like to share with you some insights I have found to help you begin to see yourself succeeding and winning at life's greatest challenges. I am convinced that there is a positive solution for every problem that could ever come your way. These solutions are found within the pages of the Bible—not just a good book, but a genuinely helpful and tremendously positive book as well.

It is tragic that so many are missing out on God's best— even Christians—because they have accepted failure, negative thinking, inferiority feelings, bad habits, and shallow faith as their way of life. They are not receiving all the good things that God has planned for them.

Jesus wants us to win at life. He promised that if we would follow Him, He would give us abundant life. I believe that abundant life is a life full of joy, full of success and satisfaction—

a contagiously happy life. He really wants us to reach our highest potential and maximize every opportunity that He gives us.

This book is my attempt to show how Jesus works in the tough areas of our lives. He doesn't turn his back and walk away when we hurt, when serious questions surface, or when every decision we make seems to be the wrong one. He really cares about each of us, and it is my desire that as you read this book, you will find the strength and encouragement to strive for the goal and live in that abundant life.

BILL WEBER

CONQUERING
REJECTION

O, what men dare do!
what men may do! what
men daily do, not knowing
what they do!

– William Shakespeare
Much Ado about Nothing

1

Rejection. Undoubtedly that word stirs up unpleasant memories, because very few people have been able to escape its powerful grip at some point in their lives.

Perhaps feelings of rejection are not just memories but a very real problem confronting you today. The rejection you feel may be left over from subtle signals you received as far back as childhood days. Someone, intentionally or not, may have indicated that you as a person were of no value. Their words, or simply their actions, told you explicitly, "I've had enough of you," "I'm tired of you," "Get away from me," or even, "Get out of my life!"

You might even encounter rejection from your own family. Many children feel rejected by parents who are either too preoccupied or simply don't care about taking an interest in them. The same is often true of spouses. There are also many parents who feel rejected by children who become so involved in other activities that they don't make time for their families. These youngsters have "tuned out" their parents, labeling them as old-fashioned and out of touch with the times. Some parents don't know how young people think or act today and feel any counsel or advice they might offer is unwanted and of little concern to their children.

Every day, there are people who feel rejection so strongly that they take the most drastic measure possible—suicide. They have had all of the rejection they can stand, and they feel that they no longer can go through life feeling so worthless. To them, death is the only escape from rejection.

Proverbs 18:14 says, "A man's spirit will endure sickness, but a broken spirit who can bear?" In other words, you can get over the measles or a cut finger or a broken arm. But a wounded spirit, hurt emotions, could cause deep emotional scars that you could carry around for the rest of your life if you don't come to grips with the problems of rejection and deal with them responsibly.

If you believe no one cares about you, then you know all too well how sharp and cutting is the emotional pain that accompanies rejection. What you may *not* know is that you do not have to feel that pain! Through the promises of God's Word, you can experience total relief from that burden of rejection and a sense of release from the emotional pain. You can learn how to be optimistic about life, regardless of how others treat you, and you can discover how to accept other people— even those you may consider enemies.

A LESSON FROM MOSES

The story of Moses begins in Exodus 2. When Moses was a baby, his mother placed him in a basket and hid him among some tall bulrushes along the banks of the Nile. She had hoped to save him from being killed by the Egyptians, who were executing all Hebrew male children. Moses was soon discovered by the daughter of the Egyptian Pharaoh when she came to bathe in the river. Full of compassion, Pharaoh's daughter took baby Moses back to the palace to raise him as her own. It was not until Moses reached adulthood that he found out his true identity. During this agonizing time, Moses saw an Egyptian mistreating a Hebrew slave, one of *his* people. In a fit of anger, he murdered the Egyptian and then fled in fear. Moses experienced horrible guilt and frustration and sought refuge in the desert, feeling rejected by God because of his terrible sin and rejected by society for his ugly behavior.

Those same feelings Moses had then are evident today in the lives of so many people. Almost assuredly, everyone has experienced some form of rejection.

Children experience it even more than sometimes realized. There is a whole generation of children who are harboring feelings of deep rejection. When parents have a child they really didn't want, that child can sense it. In anger, some parents have gone so far as to tell their child, "I wish you never had been born." Parents usually get over that feeling, but even very young children never forget it. Some older children who feel rejected may not even remember how or when that feeling originated. Other children may face rejection in school when teachers prefer some pupils over others because of race, style of dress, surface intelligence, or even behavior. Teachers who cause feelings of rejection in a child contribute to the delinquency and stir the rebellion that may already reside in that child's heart. And on the playground, children can feel rejected by their peers. Often, seemingly innocent childish taunts such as "four-eyes" or "dummy" or "fatso" can cause some psychological damage to a classmate who may already feel like a misfit.

Adults sometimes face rejection in their occupation. A colleague may have been promoted to a superior position, causing someone to feel mistreated, maligned, and hurt—rejected. Often, people who are vocationally dissatisfied are carrying rejection and hostility in their hearts from experiences that happened five or ten years earlier.

Divorce breeds a certain amount of rejection, too. With statistics showing over half of all marriages in this country ending in divorce, a lot of unhappy ex-husbands or ex-wives are feeling rejected and lonely today. Children also tend to blame them-selves when their parents break up, compounding the feelings of rejection within the family.

In fact, the most harmful and serious rejection taking place in society today is occurring within families. Rejection is being perpetrated in the home by mates, by parents, by children, and by other family members. When we feel that deep rejection from our own family, the pain and agony is as real as if we had literally been wounded.

Sadly, the problem of rejection faces Christians as well as non-Christians. Not only are believers *feeling* rejection but some are even *causing* those feelings of rejection in people around them every day. Certainly, rejection could be one of the most serious problems with which we need to deal. But rest assured, rejection can be conquered!

LOOKING FOR SYMPTOMS

How do we recognize those who feel rejected so we can offer help and acceptance?

Many who are feeling rejected are *easily hurt.* They show their feelings openly—often feelings of hostility, bitterness, or guilt. They truly don't believe they deserve good things, even when good things come their way. They feel no sense of intrinsic value whatsoever. These people have been put down so much by other people that they no longer feel of any value. They see themselves as no good—even insignificant. For these rea-sons, minority groups often feel hostile. They have felt rejection in their own environment, and some of us are guilty of having contributed to that rejection.

Others feeling rejected are likely to be *suspicious of others.* They have been "beaten down" emotionally for so long that they find it difficult to accept others who try to reach out to them in love, wanting to become their friends. They tend to think, "Now, what are they trying to get from me? Are they trying to take advantage of me?" Instead of enjoying the love and friendship offered, they try to analyze the motives behind them. This characteristic often becomes obvious in a marriage relationship. Ultimately, one of the core problems that surfaces with married couples is the feeling of rejection left over from childhood. Due to their early "programming," these people become suspicious of others, and are unwilling to accept any unconditional love that is offered. These suspicious attitudes are carried into marriage, making it difficult for them to develop deep, meaningful, lasting, and loving relationships with their spouses. They simply don't know how to handle love.

Sometimes people get out of one marriage and go into another because they felt rejection in the first. They didn't deal with that rejection responsibly, and thus never overcame it. Consequently, the second marriage also suffers or even fails because those attitudes and problems surrounding rejection have been carried over into the new relationship.

Some people who are experiencing rejection tend to *isolate themselves from others*. Remember Moses retreating to the desert? There are people today who try to escape rejection by finding ways to be alone. They try to get away from it all, sometimes even moving from one town to another to escape the rejection.

Still others practice *self-verification* when faced with rejection. These people are known for their actions which speak clearly that, "I am somebody, and I hope you know it. I am valuable. I am something special, and don't you forget it!" The problem is, they don't really believe it themselves, yet they want others to believe it. They'll choose a particular style of dress to try to impress others, thinking that even if they don't feel good about themselves, they can still "dress the part." In so doing, they hope others will recognize their significance, value, and importance. Sometimes, self-verification takes the form of perfection. People try to impress others by their performance, attempting to do everything right so they can feel they are truly worth something. Whether it is through making good grades in school or performing well on the job, outside approval is sought. Others seeking self-verification try desperately to accumulate wealth. These people believe that others would not think very highly of them if they were financially destitute— that they would be rejected as "scum of the earth." But if they were wealthy, they feel they would gain acceptance and would be regarded as more valuable to God and the rest of the world than most. There is an awesome temptation for people to be drawn into that kind of thinking. Consequently, there are masses of people who are driven to make a lot of money, even to the point of destroying their health. They will do whatever is necessary to become wealthy so they can experience self-verification, self-value, and self-worth. They feel a deep need to say, "I am now somebody because of what I have."

Other people experiencing rejection exhibit a *failure to trust in God,* even for the little things. They find it difficult to accept the fact that God loves them because of who they are, not because of what they have or haven't done. You see, God doesn't give His love to us based on what we do or don't do. He loves us all equally and wants to bless us all. But if we refuse to trust God for the "little things" and fail to recognize that He loves us as we are, then we will not be able to trust God for the "big things" in life.

REVERSE PSYCHOLOGY?

Feelings of rejection usually stem from three primary sources: experiences in our childhood, guilt, or criticism by others.

Parents often breed rejection through the disciplining of their children. Yes, children need discipline, but there is a great deal of Scripture that teaches how parents are to do it. The Bible says:

> Fathers, provoke not your children to wrath: but bring them up in the nurture and admonition of the Lord (Eph. 6:4, KJV).

This means that when we punish our children, we need to be sure that we communicate to them that we are not rejecting them as persons, but rather are rejecting only their bad behavior. We should punish them for their *actions*—bad attitudes, behavior, or habits—but not them as *persons*. We should convey to them that we love and care for them very much, but that we disapprove of their bad behavior. Too often children grow up feeling unloved, uncared for, and totally rejected because parents don't make this very important distinction when they discipline.

Some parents tend to say negative things in an attempt to motivate their children. For example, they may say, "You are never going to amount to anything," all the while hoping to motivate their child to amount to something! What they don't realize is that they are planting seeds of rejection in that child's heart, mind, and thinking that will remain with him for the rest of his life. Parents need to be wary of trying to motivate children to do good by making them feel badly. There is no justification for that "motivational" approach in the Bible.

The same goes for pastors who try to motivate their congregations to higher spiritual standards by making the church members feel shameful and sinful. Some pastors think that if they can get their congregations crawling out on their knees when the service is over, the people will turn into beautiful flowers at the end of the day. It is my contention that if they crawl out like worms, they probably are going to live like worms for the rest of the week. Sure, we all sin, but God still loves us! God wants to do something special in your life. He can turn on lights in the dark sections of your life, giving you purpose and making you bloom into something beautiful. Your life can take on vital meaning when you are responsibly related to Him.

The problem of guilt also goes hand in hand with rejection. Again, remember the example of Moses. He had killed a man and was carrying a load of guilt as he realized that he had violated something very precious. He had taken a life, and he was weighted down with the guilt of that awful deed. I believe that guilt is one of the most serious problems that we encounter in our society. Doctors tell us that one of the main reasons people are in hospitals today is because of psychosomatic-related illnesses. In other words, they have an attitude problem that has developed into a physical malfunction. I believe sincerely that if people's negative attitudes and emotional ills could be cured, a large percentage of their physical problems would not exist.

Yet, some people continue to feel badly. They feel wronged, they feel taken advantage of, and they carry that guilt around all of their lives. Because of guilt, everyone becomes suspect. They find it difficult to trust anyone. Therefore, they find it difficult to love, so they shut people out. They don't feel worthy because of the guilt of some past sin in their lives.

Listen! If you are carrying the guilt of a past sin and have not confessed that to God, confess it now and deal with it immediately. If you have already confessed that sin to God, accept that God has totally forgiven you. He has wiped that sin out of existence, and the Bible says that He remembers it no more. If God can forgive you, shouldn't you be able to forgive yourself? Carrying guilt around like a millstone in your life is one reason you may be feeling rejected. You need to deal with that problem responsibly.

Criticism of us by other people also adds to our feelings of rejection. Everyone is contributing positively or negatively to this world. We either are building up people, or we are tearing them down. We hold tremendous power in our tongues. That little part of our body, created by God as a tool of communication, can relay attitudes that destroy our families, our schools, our social lives, our businesses—whatever! Someone may say to you, "You'll never make it. You don't have what it takes." Those little words can lock into your memory, playing themselves over and over until you yourself begin to believe that you will never be able to make it.

This power to influence is a good reason that one of the

most important things we could do in our daily lives is to say to someone, "You look great. You are going to make it. You are doing a great job, and I appreciate your efforts. Keep up the good work." The Bible says:

Stir up one another to love and good works (Heb. 10:24).

That's our job! That's a command from God! It is right for us to encourage each other rather than trying to put down or destroy people with negative words.

REJECT REJECTION

To overcome feelings of rejection, first *recognize its source—* it is never from God. God does not reject you. You might say, "Oh, yes, He does. I'm sure God must reject me because of some things I have done." No! God will never reject you in that manner. In the Bible, God says:

Him that cometh to me I will in no wise cast out (John 6:37, KJV).

That's His promise—God will never reject you. Instead, He loves you, cares for you, and accepts you just as you are. You could say, "Well, I've got to clean up my act first—get rid of some bad habits and overcome some problems. Then, maybe God will take me." But God doesn't wait for that. He takes you exactly as you are, accepting you with all of your strengths, all of your problems, all of your weaknesses, all of your shame, all of the hypocrisy in your life—just *exactly* as you are.

Also, in dealing with rejection, *recognize that people are not rejecting you as a person.* In most cases, people are rejecting an action or an attitude, not an individual. If someone else at work was promoted to a job that you thought you deserved, that doesn't mean that your boss thinks you are of no value. Consider that perhaps you were not quite as prepared as your colleague at that point for the position. Be patient. Your time or your opportunity will come along soon.

A third thing you must do is *recognize that forgiveness plays a vital role in conquering rejection.* Perhaps you feel angry with your parents because they told you once that you weren't worth anything, and now you are mad at them about it. Being mad at Mom or Dad won't solve anything. Usually, what they did or said to you that made you feel rejected was out of ignorance. Few parents, if any, will intentionally try to destroy their children. Parents want what is best for their children, but there are no perfect parents. No parent knows all of the answers to all of the problems in every situation, and so mistakes will be made. If you feel rejected by your parents, simply forgive them. Don't let their mistakes continue to make you feel defeated.

Another suggestion is to *reject the rejection.* You don't have to feel rejection—just reject it! If someone rejects you, don't take it as a rejection. If someone turns away from you as if to say, "You are of no value," don't accept that. Let that attempt at rejection be the other person's problem, not yours. No one has been rejected by God, so no one should accept rejection from anyone else. If God will never reject you, you shouldn't accept rejection from others. God has accepted you, so what difference does it make if others do or do not accept you? You see, God knows all about you. The people around you— your family and friends—do not know all about you. If they reject you, it is because they have only a part of the evidence. God has all of the evidence, and He accepts you *just exactly as you are.* Ephesians 1:5 teaches:

> Having predestinated us unto the adoption of children by Jesus Christ to himself, according to the good pleasure of his will, to the praise of the glory of his grace, wherein he hath made us accepted in the beloved (kjv).

If you want to overcome this cloudy sense of self-rejection, rather than look to others for affirmation (which they may or may not give you) *look to God who made you and loves you.* Focus your relationship with Jesus Christ. God created you. He made you! You are of tremendous value because God created you and Jesus died for you to wipe away your sins. That sacrifice is what the cross is all about. Jesus gave Himself totally—He died for you—as a supreme expression of God's love for you.

The Bible tells us that God's Spirit comes to dwell in us to help us manage our lives. Why would God send us such a helper if we were of no value to Him? You *are* of value, you *are* significant, you *are* precious in the sight of God, and God totally accepts you. Instead of worrying about what men think, you should focus on your relationship with Christ. A growing spiritual dimension to your life is so important. If you rule God out of your life, you become totally dependent upon self-verification from the world. If the world doesn't give you the strokes you need, you are devastated! You have no sense of substance on which to survive. On the other hand, when you have a meaningful relationship with Christ, the whole world can turn its back on you and say you are of no value, and yet you can feel complete acceptance, worth, and love from God.

A LOVE LETTER FROM GOD

To activate this great truth, you must *learn to forgive.* If you are unforgiving toward other people, you will never get over self-rejection because you are practicing the same thing as the others. Just because they have rejected you doesn't mean you are to reject them. Forgive them! Forgiving them doesn't mean you will understand why they have done all the things they have done, or understand why they act toward you the way they act. Forgive them anyway. Make it a practice to forgive people who have rejected you or hurt you. You may say, "That's too tough to do," or "That's not practical." It is tough, all right, but not impossible. Forgiving is what Jesus Christ did for us on the cross. He is our example to forgive even our enemies.

Go one step further. *Be generous to others.* When you do

a generous deed, you are reaching through the wall that has held you in, and you are doing something positive for someone else. The Bible gives us the mandate to be generous. Luke 6:38 teaches:

> Give, and it shall be given unto you (KJV).

Many of you don't have many friends because you have no giving relationships. You only want to take. People don't care for you because you don't care for others. When you do a generous deed for someone else, it's the same as planting a seed that eventually grows and becomes a beautiful plant. The goodness comes back to you, rewarding your efforts.

Also, *keep a "clean house."* When we sin, the devil is able to convince us of our worthlessness. He says, "You know, that sin is such a small thing. You can get by with it. Nobody is going to know." Little by little, before we realize it, we disintegrate inside to the point of being hollow—just a "puff" like those fancy desserts that look pleasing and tempting on the outside but are empty on the inside. There are people who are a lot of fluff, who look like something really super and special on the outside, but when you pull back the "meringue," there's not much substance there. Their lives are like a vacuum. There is nothing there—no depth, no real values, no real purpose to their lives. Rejection ultimately can cause such emptiness.

Finally, *make the Word of God part of your life.* When you read the Bible, the words become life. Some think the Bible is a book of harsh words. They say, "I don't want to read it. It's a 'downer' to read the Bible. It makes me feel depressed." Let me encourage you to think of the Bible as a love letter from God. Perhaps you have a special box or drawer where you keep love letters tucked away as a reminder of a precious relationship. The Bible can be the most precious "love letter" you have ever received. It tells you repeatedly from beginning to end how much God loves you, accepts you, and cares for you. You'll find absolutely no rejection between its pages!

CONQUERING

ANGER

He that is slow to anger
is better than the mighty;
and he that ruleth his spirit
than he that taketh a city.

– Proverbs 16:32, KJV

2

More than 60 percent of the homicides in this nation are committed by angry family members. A medical doctor has estimated that at least fifty diseases are directly related to temperament problems. Without question, anger is serious business.

Simply because we are human beings, we have temperaments in varying forms. But of all temperaments, it is anger that seems so easily to beset us. The fact that Jesus Christ, through the power of the Holy Spirit, has come to dwell in us means that He desires to control us at that very point of our weakness. Yet, even Christian people who have been very faithful and devoted to the Lord and who have been faithful churchgoers for years have not been able to conquer their problems with anger.

We all have tempers. Temper is simply energy, and when that energy is harnessed, it can accomplish so much good. But when temper is allowed to lash out, losing its sense of direction or purpose, it can destroy, devour, and weaken us physically and spiritually. The Bible writers had much to say about the importance of bringing our tempers under control by the power of the Spirit of God. Ephesians 4:26–32 says:

> Be angry but do not sin; do not let the sun go down on your anger, and give no opportunity to the devil. Let the thief no longer steal, but rather let him labor, doing honest work with his hands, so that he may be able to give to those in need. Let no evil talk come out of your mouths, but only such as is good for edifying, as fits the occasion, that it may impart grace to those who hear. And do not grieve the Holy Spirit of God, in whom you were sealed for the day of redemption. Let all bitterness and wrath and anger and clamor and slander be put away from you, with all malice, and be kind to one another, tenderhearted, forgiving one another, as God in Christ forgave you.

A similar passage is found in Galatians 5:16–26. Again, the apostle Paul urges us to walk under the Spirit's control.

> But I say, walk by the Spirit, and do not gratify the desires of the flesh. For the desires of the flesh are against the Spirit, and the desires of the Spirit are against the flesh; for these are opposed to each other, to prevent you from doing what you would. But if you are led by the Spirit you are not under the law. Now the works of the flesh are plain: immorality, impurity, licentiousness, idolatry, sorcery, enmity, strife, jealousy, anger, selfishness, dissension, party spirit, envy, drunkenness, carousing, and the like. I warn you, as I warned you before, that those who do such things shall not inherit the kingdom of God. But the fruit of the Spirit is love, joy, peace, patience, kindness, goodness, faithfulness, gentleness, self-control; against such there is no law. And those who belong to Christ Jesus have crucified the flesh with its passions and desires. If we live by the Spirit, let us also walk by the Spirit. Let us have no self-conceit, no provoking of one another, no envy of one another.

WHAT GETS YOUR GOAT?

Ernest Leggin once said, "The measure of a man is the size of the thing that it takes to get his goat." What gets your goat? What does it take today to make you lose your self-control? Think about it. From the perspective of God's Word, we as individuals are motivated from one of two sources. We either are motivated by the flesh—our desires—or we are motivated by the Spirit. If you lose control of your temper much too easily, the Spirit of God is obviously not in control. If you often find yourself lashing out, attacking other people, selfishly clamoring for your own rights, you are being led by your own desires.

Anger is a kill-joy commonly found in our society. Few of us have not seen toddlers throw temper tantrums—they know how to put on a passionate display of anger. Young people so easily get angry with their parents or friends, and husbands and wives often get angry with each other. And when anger arises on the job, those feelings are frequently brought home to the rest of the family. It seems that for many in our society, anger has become a total way of life.

If anger is not dealt with properly during childhood, problems will often develop later in life. When children throw temper tantrums, parents frequently give in just to keep peace. As those children mature, they learn that displays of temper will probably result in their parents allowing them to have their own way. Consequently, they grow up never learning how to submit to anyone's authority. Mom and Dad can't control them, nor can teachers or principals. Government authority is meaningless, and they certainly refuse to submit to God's authority! Resisting authority has become a habit—a life pattern that is hard to break. As these rebellious youngsters move into adulthood and form family relationships of their own, they soon discover that cooperation, humility, compromise, and going the second mile are required of successful relationships. Stable marriages demand qualities of forgiveness and tolerance. But the habits are too set, the patterns too deep. When uncontrolled tempers turn into open hostility, the home is divided, often permanently. That out-of-control anger has wrecked the lives of many well-intentioned people.

Anger has been defined as "a strong feeling of irritation or displeasure; a spirit of malice that imagines and wishes the destruction of another." In the Bible, there are several words for which we substitute the word "anger," both in the Hebrew language of the Old Testament, and in the New Testament. One of the Greek words for anger is *thumas*, which means "anger of a turbulent commotion" or "a boiling agitation." This type of anger blazes up like the sudden explosion that erupts when a lit match meets a can of gasoline. Another word, *parorgismos*, means "anger that has been provoked." This type of anger is characterized by irritation or exasperation with another person. We often find ourselves at the "end of our rope" with this kind of person. *Parorgismos* is to become embittered by someone and flare up in anger. The word *orge* describes a more settled, long-lasting type of anger. It is slower to begin, but lasts longer once started. This type of anger includes revenge. *Orge* is like a pile of coals that get warmer and warmer until red hot. If they get any hotter, a white glow sets in over the coals. Many people are like that—they don't get mad easily, but when they do get angry, watch out!

Jesus Christ Himself experienced anger, but it was the type of anger we call "righteous indignation." This is the kind of attitude Jesus Christ exhibited in Mark 3:5 when "he had looked round about on them with anger . . ." (KJV). Righteous indignation often has been misunderstood. We frequently get angry at people and then defend ourselves by saying it was only "righteous indignation." In reality, it probably was "unrighteous indignation." There is a difference. Righteous indignation never is characterized by hatred, malice, or resentment toward another person. It never involves selfishness. Righteous indignation was the attitude of Jesus toward social justice. He genuinely was concerned about the treatment of God's people. He was angered by immature people who claimed to be spiritual. Jesus never got angry when anyone offended Him or took advantage of Him. Even on the cross, He did not get angry at His persecutors and lash out in retaliation. Righteous indignation, which we seldom exhibit, is so very different from unrighteous indignation, which we commonly see.

SETTING THE STAGE

To understand anger, we need to understand its stages. The first stage is *impatience,* which often results when our comfort, plans, or prestige is thwarted. Imagine a man driving into town for work and being unable to find a parking spot. He drives down an alley a block from his office and notices some trash cans next to an old building. He thinks to himself, "If I get out and move those cans, I can have my own parking spot there." He gets out of the car, moves the cans, and parks there. He is proud of himself because he has found his own "private" parking place. About six weeks later, he turns into the alley to pull into his "private" spot, but finds that someone else has discovered it! He immediately feels that someone has taken advantage of him by parking in "his" place, and an impatient attitude sets in.

Stage two can be called a *mood of anger.* Imagine that same man driving around a bit longer and discovering another parking place. But while he is getting out of his car, someone walks by and accidentally bumps his arm, causing him to drop his keys into the water drain. Now the mood of anger has set in.

Stage three occurs when a *brooding temper* begins to develop. Our frustrated friend gets to his office and notices a little breeze from the open window has blown some of his important papers onto the floor, scattering them all out of order. He begins brooding about all of the misfortunes that have taken place, then lashes out at his secretary or the first person who happens to call. He has now entered the fourth stage—*a loss of self-control.* Adults who throw temper tantrums usually look pretty silly. Their faces flush a deep red, their voices rise to a shout, and their bodies begin to sweat. The power of reason is temporarily overthrown.

Another version of this fourth stage may be even worse than a temper tantrum. It is often referred to as the "silent treatment." It is common among teenagers, and frequently used by spouses. Some husbands and wives have gone two or three weeks or more without saying a single word to each other. Others even bring a son or daughter into their little game as an intermediary—"Son, tell your mother to pass me the ketchup." Now, that's what I call losing control!

SNAP! GOES THE PATIENCE

There are a number of reasons that people lose control. One reason is because we are selfish people. One woman once told me jokingly, "I never get angry—as long as I get my way!" Joke or no joke, that attitude is too prevalent today. We want *what* we want *when* we want it.

We also get angry when we feel our rights are being violated or when we feel someone is trying to take advantage of us or mistreat us. A Christian man I know always seems to have an "issue" to discuss regarding how someone is mistreating him. He stays mad. It might be a problem with his car, his house, the community, the school, or someone on the job. He is forever irritated because he feels that people are trying to abuse him. As a result, he is usually on the very brink of losing his emotional control.

People can get angry over the silliest things. It doesn't take an international crisis to set off tempers. It can be something as simple as a shoelace breaking right in the middle of tying a shoe. As the patience snaps, the temper flares! Say you're running a few minutes late, trying to dress in a hurry, when your zipper breaks. There goes your composure! Or, downtown in heavy traffic, the light flicks from red to green but the car in front of you doesn't budge. Just see if you don't blare that horn in anger! It's amazing what Christians will do behind the wheel of a car when they're angry!

Some people find that anger can be used to manipulate

others. They find that if they become angry, others will do what they want them to do, if only to prevent a scene.

Still others use anger as a means of revenge. These people are the ones who'll say, "I'll get even with you, even if it kills me." Often, it *does* kill them because the tension of hostility builds up on the inside, destroying them emotionally, physically, and spiritually.

There is a price to pay for getting angry. In his book *None of These Diseases,* Dr. S. I. McMillen said, "The verbal expression of animosity toward others calls forth certain hormones from the pituitary, adrenal, thyroid and other glands, an excess of which can cause disease in any part of the body." [1] Anger is, indeed, serious business.

A man known in his community as an outstanding Christian was admitted to the hospital for treatment of glaucoma. His pastor came to visit him and noticed that the man was very irritated. He was furious with the doctors and nurses for not showing him enough attention, the hospital cooks for unsatisfactory food service, and the church members for not visiting him. The pastor told him, "Look, if you keep up this angry attitude, you're really going to have some serious problems." Two days later, that prediction came true when a heart attack took the life of that seventy-two-year-old man.

Anger can literally destroy us. It motivates us to hate and it creates violence. Dr. McMillen describes in his book how anger kills the joy of life:

> The moment I start hating a man, I become his slave. I can't enjoy my work anymore because he even controls my thoughts. My resentments produce too many stress hormones in my body and I become fatigued after only a few hours work. In fact, the work I formerly enjoyed is now a drudgery. Even vacations cease to give me pleasure. The man I hate finds me wherever I go. I cannot escape his tyrannical grasp upon my mind. When the waiter serves me porterhouse steak with french fries, asparagus, fresh salad, and strawberry shortcake covered with ice cream, it might as well be stale bread and water. My teeth chew the

food and I swallow it, but the man I hate will not permit me to enjoy it. The man I hate may be many miles from my bedroom, but more cruel than any slave driver. He whips my thoughts into such a frenzy that my innerspring mattress becomes a rack of torture.[2]

Anger is as contagious as an infectious germ. If you get angry at people and lash out at them, you can count on them becoming angry with you in return. Proverbs 22:24–25 says:

Make no friendship with a man given to anger, nor go with a wrathful man, lest you learn his ways and entangle yourself in a snare.

Stay away from angry people—they are contagious!

Our Christian testimony is also hindered by anger. It is impossible to be effective, joyful, radiant Christian witnesses if we are easily given to temper tantrums, for anger grieves the Holy Spirit. We are unable to operate effectively as God's children when God is disappointed in our attitude and behavior. We become spiritual pygmies with no power in our lives.

The effects of anger seem to be endless. Anger is the parent of murder. It cocks the assassin's pistol, dispenses the killer's poison, and sharpens the murder's dagger. It kindles the fire of passion, fans the flame of envy, and ultimately leaves the soul barren. But anger does not have to be a way of life. It can be conquered!

GOD-GIVEN REMEDIES

To deal most effectively with anger, we must *never repress or ignore it.* It is extremely difficult to find solutions to the problems in our lives if we continue to deny that they exist. To ignore, repress, or justify our anger is one of the worst methods of dealing with that weakness. Too often, we find it easy to rationalize our problem with anger by saying something like, "I'm Irish—what else can you expect?" or "My whole family is hot-tempered. I inherited it from my mother," or "People lose their temper sometimes. What's wrong with that?" Even worse, we may blame our temper on someone else, rather that accepting responsibility for our own feelings and actions. Rationalizing or repressing anger can lead to depression, personality disorders, critical attitudes, or general irritableness.

Instead of trying to conquer anger on your own, try some God-given remedies. First, *see anger as a sin that is condemned by God in His Word.* Until we see anger as something serious, we cannot resolve it. The Bible says in Psalm 37:8:

> Cease from anger, and forsake wrath.

In Proverbs 16:32 we are told:

> He that is slow to anger is better than the mighty; and he that ruleth his spirit than he that taketh a city (KJV).

In James 1:19 the Bible says:

> Wherefore, my beloved brethren, let every man be swift to hear, slow to speak, slow to wrath (KJV).

And in Proverbs 14:17 we find:

> He that is soon angry dealeth foolishly (KJV).

Next, *confess anger to God honestly as a sin.* Until you confess your anger before God, you will not be cured. We often revere Moses as a biblical hero. But even Moses had a problem with anger. When he brought the Ten Commandments down from Mount Sinai, he lost control of his temper when he saw the people disobeying God. He threw down the stone tablets in a fury, and God had to give him the Ten Commandments a second time. On another occasion, Moses was told by God to speak to a rock, from which water would flow to quench the thirst of the Israelites in the desert. But Moses lost his temper, and he struck the rock with his staff instead. Because of that angry action, he forfeited the right to enter the Promised Land of Canaan.

Third, *ask God to take away the habit of becoming angry.*

Anger can develop into a serious pattern. To overcome it, we must ask God to help us. We have had too much practice throughout the years in becoming angry for the problem to just disappear. We need supernatural help to create a gentle spirit in its place. As 1 John 5:14–15 says:

And this is the confidence which we have in him, that if we ask anything according to his will he hears us. And if we know that he hears us in whatever we ask, we know that we have obtained the requests made of him.

Fourth, *never encourage or prolong the state of anger once you have fallen into it.* Apologize quickly, for the Bible says:

Come to terms quickly with your enemy before it is too late . . . (Matt. 5:25, TLB).

It also tells us:

Do not let the sun go down on your anger (Eph. 4:26).

Still another Bible command says:

So if you are offering your gift at the altar, and there remember that your brother has something against you, leave your gift there before the altar and go; first be reconciled to your brother, and then come and offer your gift (Matt. 5:23–24).

Fifth, *ask God to make you a peacemaker rather than an agitator.* You are one or the other, not both. You are either bringing more peace into a fellowship or more diversion. No one can be neutral in this regard. The Bible says:

Blessed are the peacemakers, for they shall be called the children of God (Matt. 5:9, KJV).

If we are to overcome this problem with anger in our lives, we need to pray: *Dear Lord, help me to be a peacemaker. Help me to be a spiritual catalyst who can help solve problems* and bring people together and calm the rough waters that rage in the lives and souls of others.

Finally, *thank God that through the help of His Holy Spirit He is changing us into this patient, loving, forgiving, peaceable kind of person.* Let Jesus Christ do in your life what He would like to do. Let Him move into your heart and take control of your temper through the power of His Holy Spirit. With God's help, you can conquer it!

CONQUERING

RESENTMENT

Nothing on earth
consumes a man more quickly
than the passion of resentment.

– Friedrich Nietzsche
Ecce Home

3

Have you ever held a grudge against someone? I don't think there is a person anywhere who could answer "No." I am convinced that the spirit of resentment is one of the most deadly viruses running rampant in our society today.

Because we are human, we tend to harbor resentment against those who we feel have wronged us. We don't always react and respond to others or to situations as we should. Instead, we become resentful.

The New Testament church in Ephesus undoubtedly had some of the same problems with feelings of resentment. The message of instruction and encouragement which Paul sent to those church members is a personal and practical message for us, as well. Look at the apostle's words in Ephesians 4:22–30:

> Put off your old nature which belongs to your former manner of life and is corrupt through deceitful lusts, and be renewed in the spirit of your minds, and put on the new nature, created after the likeness of God in true righteousness and holiness.

Therefore, putting away falsehood, let every one speak the truth with his neighbor, for we are members one of another. Be angry but do not sin; do not let the sun go down on your anger, and give no opportunity to the devil. Let the thief no longer steal, but rather let him labor, doing honest work with his hands, so that he may be able to give to those in need. Let no evil talk come out of your mouths, but only such as is good for edifying, as fits the occasion, that it may impart grace to those who hear. And do not grieve the Holy Spirit of God, in whom you were sealed for the day of redemption.

And in verses 31–32, Paul gives us this command:

Let all bitterness and wrath and anger and clamor and slander be put away from you, with all malice, and be kind to one another, tenderhearted, forgiving one another, as God in Christ forgave you.

Without a doubt, resentment runs rampant, and not even Christians are exempt from its effects. No one has gone through life without experiencing resentment or carrying a grudge toward another. This "virus" is poisonous and deadly, creeping upon us, often consuming us before we realize what is happening. Resentment is deadly because it destroys relationships among people who ought to know better. It is poisonous in that it robs us of inner peace and serenity. Resentment tends to make us hard and bitter—at times even antagonistic toward others who we feel have hurt or offended us. A friend once described resentment like this: "It is the sticking of needles into your bare breast, hoping this will make the other fellow hurt. It is where you punish yourself, hoping that the other person will suffer as a result." [1]

A pastor friend of mine told of a time he made a routine visit to an elderly lady in his congregation. This woman had been faithful in her church attendance, yet he had observed throughout the years that she seemed to be in a constant state of inner turmoil. He couldn't quite put his finger on the problem, but he knew something was troubling her.

During their idle conversation that day, the pastor commented about a wanted criminal who had just been captured. That man was eighty years old at the time of his arrest. As the pastor mentioned this criminal, the woman began to glare at him. "Now, answer this," she retorted angrily. "That eighty-year-old man is a reprobate. He is a criminal not worth anything. Yet he has lived all of these years anyway. Would you please tell me why my husband, who was a wonderful Christian, died at the age of forty-one? Why did that happen to him?"

For the first time, the pastor realized what had been bothering this woman all these years. She had been harboring a spirit of resentment ever since her husband's death. She resented God for taking her husband from her. She resented all men who were older than her husband. She even resented women who were able to have their husbands with them for many years. Throughout her life, she had been nursing that pain and nurturing an attitude of resentment within her heart.

"GOD MEANT IT FOR GOOD"

The Old Testament book of Genesis tells the beautiful story of a young man named Joseph. Joseph was the favorite son of his father, Jacob. As a gift of love, his father presented Joseph with a special coat—a coat we have come to know as his "coat of many colors." Joseph was also a dreamer, and his dreams angered his jealous brothers, who plotted to kill him. One day, they threw him into a deep pit, intending to let him die. But some Midianite traders passed by, and Joseph's brothers decided to sell him instead. The traders took him to Egypt, where Joseph became a slave in the house of Potiphar, the captain of Pharaoh's guards.

For thirteen years Joseph was kept in captivity, but even in those circumstances he tried to do God's will. He fled temptation when Potiphar's wife tried to seduce him. Angry at his rejection, she accused Joseph of attacking her and had him thrown into prison. Seemingly an unfair thing for God to allow, wasn't it? Joseph had taken a stand for what was good and right—that which was the will of God—and yet was persecuted, placed in captivity, thrown in prison.

Joseph easily could have felt resentful toward his brothers or toward God. But there is no indication that Joseph ever indulged in an attitude of resentment. He was later brought before Pharaoh and successfully interpreted Pharaoh's dreams. Because of Joseph's faithfulness and discernment, Pharaoh made him ruler over all of Egypt, second only to Pharaoh himself. Years later, his brothers came to him to buy grain during the severe famine which he had predicted. Joseph tested them, and then revealed himself with compassion toward these same brothers who had sold him into slavery. When they came before him, he told them, "Fear not, for am I in the place of God? . . . you meant evil against me; but God meant it for good" (Gen. 50:19–20). Joseph showed a spirit of love and forgiveness, rather than resentment.

The average person, however, is touchy, self-centered, egotistical, and has an unsurrendered self-will. We are more concerned about our personal rights than about the rights of other people. We want our own way, so our relationships with others tend to reflect a selfish attitude and a jealous disposition. We want to get ahead, even if it means stepping on someone else to do it.

Perhaps we are resentful when financial or professional success comes to others, rather than to us. Feelings of resentment can lead to scores of other negative attitudes, including envy, anger, and jealousy. But, like Joseph, we can conquer resentment with God's help.

One man I know of felt he was in line for a promotion, but when the higher position came open, the management brought in an outsider for the job. Immediately, the man became angry, emotionally devastated, bitter, and full of wrath. His indignation and resentment boiled up inside toward the man who got the job instead of him.

A Christian co-worker recognized what his friend was feeling and suggested that he swallow his pride, go across the hall and introduce himself to the new boss, offer congratulations to him, and seek ways to help him in any way possible. The resentful man, himself a Christian, realized that he had been given good advice. He pulled himself together, walked across the hall and made himself available to the new boss. As a result, a very beautiful and meaningful relationship developed. Two years went by, and the boss was transferred again. This time, the man was promoted to that coveted position. His superiors told him they had been impressed with his cooperative, loving spirit during the previous two years and wanted to reward him with the position. As this example shows, we need to keep our negative attitudes under control because we never know when we are being watched by others.

TRUTH OR CONSEQUENCES

As Paul reminds us in Galatians 6:7, we sow what we reap. If we sow seeds of bitterness and resentment, we have to suffer the consequences for nursing those attitudes within us. Doctors tell us that rashes, hives, and even ulcers often are created by a spirit of resentment which people let develop within them. One doctor remarked that resentment and anger put the whole physical and mental system in a state of war, rather than a state of peace. Surely you have heard someone exclaim, "That person just burns me up!" How true that is. We often allow our feelings to fester inside, creating real physical problems. Not only do anger and resentment affect our physical well-being, but they affect our physical perspective, as well. Eye doctors will verify that anger can narrow the field of vision and shut off the peripheral vision. Consequently, it is dangerous to drive when angry, because you can't clearly see things that are not in the direct line of vision. I'm sure you've heard someone say, "That makes me so mad, I can't see straight!" Again, how true that is. Resentment, bitterness, wrath, anger—they all affect our physical functioning and well-being.

They also affect us emotionally and spiritually. Those feelings of resentment can rob us of close fellowship with God. We become inefficient or ineffective in our jobs, and we find it impossible to witness the love of God and the power of Jesus Christ when we harbor a grudge or a spirit of resentment within our hearts.

What do we do when we feel resentful? Let's look first at what not to do. *Don't feel obligated to express that resentment by just throwing it all out in the open.* A woman once told me, "I wish that just one time—just one time—I could tell my husband where to go. I think if I could just get that off my chest one time. . . ." This way of dealing with resentment won't solve anything. It's been tried, and it doesn't work.

We cannot suppress resentment by just keeping it hidden beneath the surface. We think that if we just keep going, no one will ever know. Of course, this attitude doesn't solve anything either. You don't cure a boil by placing a bandage on top of it. It has to be lanced before it can heal. The same goes with our emotions. We need to recognize our problems and deal with them—not simply try to cover them up.

Nor can we try to overcome our resentment by taking out our anger on someone else. If you have a bad experience at work, it's tempting to come home and take out your frustrations on the dog, your husband or wife, or even the children. This attitude never solves the problem.

And it is impossible to deal with a spirit of resentment by nursing it along. Many people carry grudges against people for fifteen, twenty, even thirty years or longer. Periodically, they take out that old resentment and mull it over in their minds, recalling all of the bitterness once experienced. Again, this solves nothing. But the truth is that we don't have to let resentment ruin our relationships, our health, or our lives.

WAR IN THE MONKEY KINGDOM

God's Word has some specific and definite words of instruction on how to deal with this serious problem. If you are overcome by feelings of resentment, first *recognize that all resent-*

ment is sin. Without a doubt, it is wrong to harbor resentment—it never is justified and needs always to be confessed. The problem with many of us is that we tend to justify or rationalize our resentment, but there is no justification. Resentment is sin, and it needs to be confessed in order to experience the day-by-day fellowship of God.

Titus 3:3 tells us:

> For we ourselves were once foolish, disobedient, led astray, slaves to various passions and pleasures, passing our days in malice and envy, hated by men and hating one another.

You see, we never resolve bitterness by hating other people. Hate never solved anything.

I once heard a missionary to India tell of watching monkeys fight in the jungle. He said, "It is amazing how typical monkeys are as compared to relationships of human beings who get angry with one another." As he observed the jungle monkeys, he noted a pattern emerging. First, one monkey caught the eye of another and started glaring at it. Next, the monkey made a face, bared his teeth, and began to growl, louder and louder. Finally, the monkey jumped up and down, turning around in circles. As the other monkey watched, it also became mad and imitated the same routine. The monkeys then started making dashes at each other, running back and forth, becoming more and more angry, getting closer and closer to each other until one of the monkeys finally "stepped over the line" and was struck by the other. In this monkey kingdom, war has been declared.

As silly as that may sound, we're not too different from those monkeys when it comes to resentment. Human beings also go through stages of developing resentments, hatred, anger, and wrath toward one another. And, like those monkeys, the more intensely we hate, the more intensely we are hated.

To overcome this problem, we should not only confess resentment as sin, but as Paul tells us in 1 Timothy 2:8, we need to *make it a matter of prayer:*

I desire then that in every place the men should pray, lifting holy hands without anger or quarreling.

A true test of our maturity is the way we respond when someone has offended us. According to the Bible, our response should be to pray for those who come against us.

"HELP ME NOT TO HATE"

During World War II, Captain George Barondise was a skipper of a beautiful luxury liner. Leaving his ship anchored in Rotterdam, Holland, Captain Barondise vacationed on another ship bound for New York, where he planned to visit friends. While crossing the Atlantic Ocean, the passengers and crew received word that Rotterdam had been bombed by the Germans. A third of the city had been destroyed, including Captain Barondise's beloved ship.

He immediately thought of his wife and son, but had no way of finding out if they were safe. Yet he still prayed this prayer, "God, no matter what happens, help me not to hate. Please guide the thoughts, words, and actions of those who rule over these countries at war. May Your will be done, and Your kingdom come." Then Captain Barondise slowly added this plea, "God, watch over my wife and son. Before my wife was mine, she belonged to You. Before my little boy came to me, he was Yours. They are in Your hands, Father. I trust You." He paused, and then prayed, "And Lord, help me not to hate Hitler. Help me to mean that, O God." [2]

Here was a man in the midst of a situation in which most of us would feel strong resentment toward someone who had destroyed our livelihood, our home, and possibly even our family. Yet Captain Barondise prayed for his attitude and response to that crisis. Imagine his incredible joy when he finally discovered that his family had escaped the destruction unharmed!

Not only should we learn to pray for ourselves, but we should also learn to *pray for the person who has offended us.* As Jesus said in Matthew 5:44:

> Love your enemies and pray for those who persecute you.

It is impossible to maintain bitterness toward someone if you are praying for him at the same time. You need the prayer for your sake, and that person needs your prayers, as well, to be liberated and strengthened.

The Bible also teaches us to *forgive those against whom we feel resentment.* In 1 John 4:7 we find the command:

> Beloved, let us love one another: for love is of God; and every one that loveth is born of God, and knoweth God (kjv).

If God so loved us, we should also love one another.

Abraham Lincoln once reprimanded a young army officer for indulging in violent controversy with one of his associates. Lincoln advised the young soldier, "No man who is resolved to make the most of himself can afford to spare time for personal contention." Forgive the person that has offended you and then take it a step further. *Show acts of kindness toward the very person you once resented.* As Hebrews 12:14 tells us:

> Strive for peace with all men, and for the holiness without which no one will see the Lord.

In 1 Thessalonians 5:14 Paul tells us:

> And we exhort you, brethren, admonish the idlers, encourage the fainthearted, help the weak, be patient with them all.

In Romans 12:20 we are taught:

> Feed your enemy if he is hungry. If he is thirsty give him something to drink and you will be "heaping coals of fire on his head." In other words, he will feel ashamed of himself for what he has done to you (tlb).

Notice carefully verse 21:

> Don't let evil get the upper hand, but conquer evil by doing good.

Our natural inclination is to do everything but what these Scriptures teach. If we are offended, we feel that we must offend in return. If someone takes advantage of us, we feel we must get even by taking advantage of them in return. But as Christians, we are taught to respond to evil with love.

RESTORING LOST LOVE

A woman once told her counselor, "I cannot stand my husband, and I want to be as mean as I can to him." The counselor replied, "All right. If you want to be mean to your husband, here's what you do. Go home and tell your husband that you love him. Do everything possible to prove it. Do things that you have never thought to do for him before, and then when he is convinced you love him more than anybody else in the world, tell him you do not love him any longer and you want a divorce." She said, "I'll do it."

In a few weeks, she came back with the report that she had followed her counselor's advice. "Very good. Now sue for divorce," the counselor said. The woman looked at the counselor incredulously. "Are you crazy?" she asked. "I've fallen in love with my husband for the first time in years. Our marriage is more beautiful than it has ever been."

Making something positive out of negative circumstances is a major step in conquering resentment. Concentrate on finding that silver lining every time a cloud of adversity comes your way. I guarantee that you'll live a much happier life.

Talking about your feelings of resentment with a Christian friend or a Christian counselor also will help in overcoming the problem. Seek their perspective and advice, and be willing to follow it through.

Consider working out frustration and anger through *physical activity*. Pent-up feelings can be worked out through a simple physical exercise routine. A doctor once asked a remarkable sixty-year-old man what he had been doing to keep so physically fit. The man replied, "My wife and I agreed years ago when we were first married that if one of us was in a bad mood, I would take a long walk to let tempers cool down. Frankly, doctor, much of my life has been spent outdoors. The sun and the breeze have been so healthy for me." Oftentimes, working out, hiking, playing sports or participating in other physical exercise can be among the most refreshing things we can do for ourselves as we work through our resentment.

Also, *try practicing some understanding and imagination* when encountering feelings of resentment. Put yourself in the other person's shoes and try to understand what makes him or her tick. Consider the problems he or she is facing. When we understand other people's problems, we usually are more patient with them.

Finally, *use resentment as a teacher.* When problems come, remember that God is sovereign and He often permits problems to come into our lives to teach us something. Right now, you could be in conflict with members of your family or business associates, or perhaps a neighbor. In the midst of this difficulty, God could be trying to teach you a lesson about Himself or about His will for your life. Or, He could be showing you some area of weakness in your daily living. Rather than resisting God, open yourself up to Him so that He can restore love in your heart—and teach you a valuable lesson at the same time.

A Christian farmer in India was harvesting his crops one day when he was attacked by several vicious men. They took an axe and chopped off the ends of his fingers. Before they left, they stole all of his crops. When the villagers heard what happened, they took up a collection so the man could prosecute his attackers. When they presented the money to him, the farmer told them, "You know, I am a new Christian, and when I invited Jesus Christ into my heart, I made a promise. I said that I would follow Jesus Christ as my Master and my Lord. I would be the kind of person He wants me to be. When Jesus Christ was hanging on the cross two thousand years ago after men persecuted Him and even put Him to death,

He did not say that they ought to be punished because of what they had done. Rather, He said, 'Father, forgive them, for they know not what they do.' Because that same Jesus is my Jesus and He lives in me, rather than prosecuting these men I want to forgive them. They do not realize what they have done. They have acted in ignorance." [3]

Here is a man who has learned how to handle resentment. How reassuring to know that we can, too—with the help of our Lord.

CONQUERING

STRESS

The bow too tensely strung
is easily broken.

– Publilius Syrus

4

Americans are more prone to tenseness and stress than any other people on earth. We have for decades been on the fore-front of new scientific discoveries and technical inventions to make life "easier," but still the endless pressures of our hurried lives make us prone to more heart attacks and tension head-aches. A visiting nineteenth-century French author once wrote and told his countrymen that an American had "invented a chair called a rocking chair, in which he can move while he sits." We have been called the "uptight generation," and rightly so. This is indeed,

> The age of the half-read page
> And the quick hash and the mad dash.
> The bright night and the nerves tight,
> The plane hop, the brief stop,
> The brain strain and the heart pain.
> The cat naps till the spring snaps,
> And the fun's done.[1]

We Americans wear too much expression on our faces. We are living with all our nerves in action. We live in such a pressure-packed age that life's problems no longer seem to be simple, and answers are hard to come by. Responsible decisions and actions are demanded, yet we often feel a lack of time and ability to deal responsibly with those problems and pressures.

Those in the business world live with tension daily. One businessman was so overwhelmed with the tension, frustration, and turmoil that he sought advice from his pastor. As they talked, the man chain-smoked, fidgeted, and kept rubbing his chin nervously. Even the pastor's advice to "slow down" brought the man more tension. "I know I need to unwind, but I just can't right now," he said. "With all of the economic problems in my line of business, I'm under so much pressure to succeed that I honestly don't know how to slow down and end this rat race." His frustration is typical of that faced by many other professionals in the business community. This man is the norm, not the exception.

Those who work in the home don't escape tension and frustration, either. A housewife recently went to her doctor, with complaints of feeling run down. After a thorough examination, the doctor told her, "Lady, you're not run down. You're too wound up."

Even children are affected by tension. A little girl once told her mother that she was nervous. "Honey, what do you mean?" the mother asked. "I really don't know, but I just feel in a hurry all over," the little girl replied. It seems that no particular age group or profession is exempt from the high pressures of today's society.

HARNESSING STRESS

Stress doesn't have to be all bad. Tension can play a positive and vital role in our daily living—if we can learn how to manage it properly. Speakers who understand creative tension can add dynamics to their presentation. Athletes can excel far beyond their normal capabilities when faced with a trying set of circumstances. Sales representatives can stay ahead of sales resistance. In his book *A Study of History,* Arnold Toynbee notes that the unrelenting pressure of necessity stirs the creative powers and brings out the greatness in humankind.[2]

For stress to have positive value, however, it must be temporary. Those who allow tension to be an ever-present emotion in everyday life are inviting a powerful, destructive force to reign within them. Is the stress in your life temporary, or is it slowly destroying your life? Try the following test, answering each question as honestly as you can. Your answers could determine whether or not you are overly tense.

1. Do minor problems throw you into a dither?
2. Do you find it difficult to get along with people, develop friendships, or begin conversations with others?
3. Do the small pleasures of life fail to satisfy you?
4. Do you find it difficult or impossible to stop thinking about your personal anxieties?
5. Do you fear new people and situations?
6. Are you suspicious of other people or mistrust your friends?
7. Have you picked up any bad, dangerous, or destructive habits that you have been unable to shake?

If you answered "yes" to most of the questions, you are probably finding it difficult to deal with a tension-ridden society. As stress and tension become a way of life, you will find that other people will not want to be around you because you have become uptight and nervous. You are no longer enjoyable to be around, and you will find that others will quickly cut off conversations with you or try to avoid you.

Tension not only can affect your relationship with others, but it can also affect you personally and physically. Dr. Herbert Vincent of the Harvard Medical School tells what effects stress has on our bodies:

. . . there is an increase within the body of a hormone called adrenaline. This, in turn, increases the blood pressure—that is, the amount of blood flowing into the muscles—and the rate of the heartbeat, causes excessive sweating, headaches and an upset stomach. This can create a 'fight or flight' response with the body. So, if you want to suffer the side results—possibly heart attack, premature death, stomach disorders, high blood pressure, nervous difficulties—you continue down the road of uptightness and tenseness.[3]

THE LADDER TO SUCCESS . . . AND STRESS

It is difficult for us to function normally when under stress. An experienced actor under a lot of pressure will forget his lines. In a moment of tension, a capable and well-qualified golf professional will miss a twelve-inch putt. During a crucial play, a star halfback will fumble the ball. An experienced preacher who is under a great deal of stress will forget his text. It is disturbing, even embarrassing, to discover that we cannot cope with stress and tension in a responsible way.

Stress, contrary to popular belief, is not caused primarily by overwork. William James once said, "Neither the nature nor the amount of our work is accountable for the frequency and the severity of our breakdowns. Their cause lies rather in the absurd feeling of hurry and having no time, in breathlessness and tension and anxiety." [4] John Wesley, a great Methodist preacher, arose at four o'clock every morning and often preached up to five times a day. In fifty years of ministry, he preached more than forty thousand times, which averages fifteen sermons a week! He traveled more than 250 thousand miles to spread the gospel.[5] Yet, he never hurried, he never worried, and he never suffered the wear and tear of stress.

You see, the body is constructed to work, but it is not constructed to endure severe strain or prolonged tension. In fact, each of us has a specific fatigue limit. We reach a certain point where life's pressures, circumstances, and experiences are so overwhelming that we feel we can no longer cope. But in our all-out effort to climb the ladder of success, we often ignore the warning signs of stress. Such symptoms can include migraines, high blood pressure, frequent colds, and, at the extreme, even strokes or heart attacks.

The sheer "noise factor" within American society often causes stress. Prolonged exposure to noise can cause severe stress symptoms, leading to chronic effects such as hypertension or ulcers. Often the sounds of today's world are rasping and shrill, generally irritating to our sense of calm and well-being. Televisions, radios, stereos, traffic, telephones, doorbells, lawn mowers, typewriters, whatever—noise is inevitable and can create unrelenting tension, both emotionally and physically.

A strong desire to succeed economically is another major contributor to stress. The highly competitive spirit which many of us have can create unhealthy ambitions. We want to get ahead, be successful, do well financially. Our "get results" culture has created a step-lively, don't-block-the-traffic attitude that can be quite damaging as tension and stress build up within.

We feel the pressure socially, as well. We are the true American status seekers. We surely don't want others to think we have less or know less than they do. So we go through all sorts of tricks trying to "keep up with the Joneses." We want to wear the right clothes, drive the right cars, live in the right neighborhoods. We use upper class vocabularies and are sure to throw in the appropriate clichés of the day. This "one-upmanship" is quite common as a stress factor in today's society.

There is a story about two French poodles who were strutting along the sidewalk one day, freshly groomed with cute ribbons around their necks, feeling quite feisty. Turning a corner, they met a scraggly little mutt. One of the poodles pawed the ground, sniffed the air and said, "My name is Mimi, spelled M-i-m-i." The second poodle then scratched the ground and threw back her head, saying, "My name is Fifi, spelled F-i-f-i." Not to be outdone, the little mutt pawed the ground with all four legs, stuck his nose in the air, and said, "My name is Fido, spelled P-h-y-d-e-a-u-x."

A silly story, perhaps, but so strikingly similar to the way many of us act today. We are fearful of losing our status if anyone should get ahead of us in anything. It's all a game— and one that creates a great deal of stress and tension as we strive to stay ahead.

WINNING THE BATTLE AGAINST STRESS

Perhaps one of the most basic causes of stress and tension is the failure to possess or practice a personal faith in Jesus Christ. Many people are substituting religious games for true spiritual experiences. One of the first steps in overcoming tension is to *put Christ in the center of your life.* If you are truly serious about overcoming stress, you must make a personal commitment of faith and trust in Jesus Christ as your Lord and Savior. Winning the battle with stress begins here.

There is no way that Christ can be the center of your life if you do not trust Him to forgive you of your sins and give you a quality of life that will endure. He is not someone to simply "add on" to your life. By placing Him in control of your life, He can be free to direct your life to realize its full potential, virtually free from damaging anxiety and stress. The apostle Paul once said that he could "do all things in him who strengthens me" (Phil. 4:13). Paul had spent many years in prison and had often been mistreated. He obviously had every reason to be tense, frustrated, and uptight. Yet he recognized the value of having Jesus Christ as his personal guide, offering strength to deal with all of life's troubles.

Psalm 87:7 tells us:

All my springs are in thee (KJV).

When people are rightly related to Christ, they have a central purpose for living. One of the reasons people so often feel confused and anxious is that they really do not know why they are living. Christ must become that central purpose in life.

Not only should you make a personal commitment to Christ,

but you also need to learn to *thank God for every experience that comes into your life.* Rather than letting adverse situations create tension, thank God for them. Paul tells us in 1 Thessalonians 5:18:

> In every thing give thanks: for this is the will of God in Christ Jesus concerning you.

If Christ is to be the center of your life, it is essential that you *trust the promises of His Word.* The Word of God is full of encouragement and positive affirmations for tense and anxious people. Through studying God's Word, we can learn to cope with the pressures of life. Deuteronomy 33:27 teaches:

> The eternal God is thy refuge, and underneath are the everlasting arms (KJV).

Psalm 121:1 says:

> I will lift up mine eyes unto the hills, from whence cometh my help (KJV).

Psalm 46:1 tells us:

> God is our refuge and strength, a very present help in trouble (KJV).

And Isaiah 40:30-31 says:

> Even the youths shall faint and be weary, and the young men shall utterly fall: But they that wait upon the LORD shall renew their strength; they shall mount up with wings as eagles; they shall run, and not be weary; and they shall walk, and not faint (KJV).

Take heed of a modernized version of the 23rd Psalm:

> The Lord is my pacesetter, I shall not rush. He makes me stop and rest for quiet intervals. He provides me with images of stillness which restore my serenity. He leads me in the ways of efficiency through calmness of mind, and his guidance is peace. Even though I have a great many things to accomplish each day, I will not fret, for his presence is here. His timelessness,

his all-importance will keep me in balance. He prepares refreshment and renewal in the midst of my activity. By anointing my head with his oils of tranquility, my cup of joyous energy overflows. Surely harmony and effectiveness shall be the fruits of my hours. For I shall walk in the pace of my Lord and dwell in his house forever.[6]

Is the Lord truly your pacesetter? Take an honest look at your life and activities. Analyze how you are spending your time on a daily basis. Ask yourself these questions: *Will it make any difference six months from now? Will the decision I make today—the way I spend my time—make any difference six months from now?* One woman who did this found that she was so busy running from club meeting to club meeting, from bridge table to canasta game, from luncheon to luncheon, that she had no time left to do anything that really mattered. From that moment on, she reorganized her life.

A heart-attack victim had a similar experience after spending two months in a hospital bed. "I have had time to really analyze my life," he said, "and I am going to change my priorities. I am going to change the way I use my time. Life is too short to waste with things that are not meaningful."

JUST TEN MINUTES A DAY

Take time each day for thinking and quiet meditation. Have you discovered the importance of getting alone every day for quiet thought? Life demands periods of quietness in which we can slow down and drop our "buckets" into the wells of power and peace. Henry Drummond has said that he could manage the hurry and rush of anything fate could bring if he could take ten minutes of the day to be thoughtfully aware of God. In those ten minutes, he can clear away any clutter and eliminate the unimportant. That meditation allows him to see clearly the course he is to follow, and he finds resources for strength through this brief quiet time with God.[7]

Blaise Pascal, the French philosopher, physicist, and mathematician, once said, "All the evils of life have fallen upon us because men will not sit quietly in a room. We have got to be doing something, going somewhere or talking to someone." The Old Testament psalmist also admonishes us to hear God's plea written in Psalm 46:10:

Be still, and know that I am God.

If you are to conquer stress, you need to *give your body plenty of rest and relaxation.* Jesus knew the importance of rest. In Mark 6:30, He tells His disciples to "come aside and rest." There is something important, meaningful, inspirational, and uplifting about rest and relaxation.

It is just as important to *take up some form of physical activity or become interested in a hobby.* Golf, tennis, jogging, swimming, or a variety of other activities will help you burn up some of the destructive energy within, relieving tension and allowing you to relax.

You also need to take time to *plan your work daily.* Are your time and energy wisely spent? Planning ahead can eliminate wasted time and make you feel more productive, thus helping to reduce stress.

Also, *develop an attitude of acceptance* when contrary or seemingly unmanageable circumstances come your way. There are some things that are going to happen no matter what you do, or no matter how much faith you have. Rather than resisting, fighting, or becoming uptight about those circumstances, learn to accept them and cooperate with the inevitable. Make your plans, but allow a degree of flexibility. Jesus encountered numerous unknowns along the road of life. Often, as He went His way to preach, interruptions came. Rather than becoming tense about the distractions, Jesus accepted the interruptions and turned them into opportunities for ministry.

ONE DAY AT A TIME

If at all possible, try to *live only one day at a time.* As the psalmist said:

This is the day which the Lord has made; let us rejoice and be glad in it (Psalm 118:24).

These twenty-four hours may be the last twenty-four hours that God allows you to live. Learn to enjoy and appreciate it, living it to its fullest.

It will help, too, if you can *develop a good sense of humor.* One of the healthiest and most spiritual things we can do is to have a good laugh and share a good smile. Laughter is one of the best escape valves for a pent-up spirit. R. M. Vincent said, "God gave us humor to save us from going mad." Abraham Lincoln once took a book from his shelf and read several jokes to his Cabinet before their meeting, saying afterward, "I should die if I did not laugh occasionally." The Bible tells us in Proverbs 17:22:

A cheerful heart is a good medicine.

One final suggestion—*ask God to help you discipline and control your ambitions.* Some of the goals we have set for ourselves perhaps are beyond our abilities, beyond our capacities, and beyond what represents God's will for our lives. Rather than becoming tense and uptight about our inabilities, let us ask God to give us strength, wisdom, and understanding of what He wants us to accomplish. Then as we put our shoulders to the task of day-by-day living, we will know that we are not trying to fulfill selfish motivations. Instead, we will be sincerely trying to fulfill the will of God in our lives. Only then can we truly be calm in this very tense, stressful world.

CONQUERING
_A_
POOR SELF-IMAGE

It is difficult to
make a man miserable while
he feels worthy of himself and
claims kindred to the great
God who made him.

– Abraham Lincoln

5

When you arise each morning and look at yourself in the mirror, do you like the person you see? In many cases, the answer would be a resounding "No!"

I am convinced that one of the most significant reasons that people are unable to develop a meaningful faith in God or meaningful relationships with other people is that they do not have an appreciation for who they are—one of God's very special creations! If we do not like ourselves, it is very difficult for anyone else to like us.

The people whom God used most effectively to make a dramatic impact on our world were people who had good self-images of themselves. King David was such a man. He was human in every respect—he sinned, but he was forgiven by God. He came to understand what God was trying to accomplish in his life, and through that experience, he began to feel much better about himself. We see his reflections in Psalm 139:1–6.

O LORD, thou has searched me and known me! Thou knowest when I sit down and when I rise up; thou discernest my thoughts from afar. Thou searchest out my path and my lying down, and art acquainted with all my ways. Even before a word is on my tongue, lo, O LORD, thou knowest it altogether. Thou dost beset me behind and before, and layest thy hand upon me. Such knowledge is too wonderful for me; it is high, I cannot attain it.

In Psalm 139:13–18, David has this conversation with the Lord:

For thou didst form my inward parts, thou didst knit me together in my mother's womb. I praise thee, for thou art fearful and wonderful. Wonderful are thy works! Thou knowest me right well; my frame was not hidden from thee, when I was being made in secret, intricately wrought in the depths of the earth. Thy eyes beheld my unformed substance; in thy book were written, every one of them, the days that were formed for me, when as yet there was none of them. How precious to me are thy thoughts, O God! How vast is the sum of them! If I would count them, they are more than the sand. When I awake, I am still with thee.

In his book *Hide and Seek,* psychologist James Dobson said, "I've observed that the vast majority of those people between the ages of twelve and twenty years are bitterly disappointed with who they are and what they represent." [1] How sad that more of us today do not experience the joy that comes from having a positive self-image, as did David.

ARE YOU HAPPY WITH YOU?

In a recent survey, groups of high school students were asked three questions: *What would you do to change your appearance to be more acceptable to others? What abilities do you wish that you had that you do not have? Why do you feel rejected, if you feel that you are?* Here is a sampling of their answers to those questions: too fat, too skinny, too tall, too short, big nose, uncoordinated, bowlegged, bad voice, big feet, skinny legs, fat legs, close-set eyes, acne, big ears, pigeon-toed, scars, no chest, deformed, bad teeth, poor eyes, poor hair.

Most people would like to change something about themselves. Few of us are ever satisfied with our appearance. But God loves us just the way we are, and He made us in a very special way. If we can accept the way God made us, we will be willing to trust God for many other decisions and plans for our lives. But if we can't accept ourselves, we will have difficulty relating to other people, responding well to authority, or developing healthy friendships, marriages, and business relationships. Why? Because no one likes to be around people who are always putting themselves down. This avoidance can lead to loneliness and rejection—even depression. In addition, you'll have trouble with God. In a sense, you are saying, "God, You really blew it when You made me. If You were such a great God, You wouldn't have made me look the way I look."

The Pharisees once asked Jesus, "What do you think is the greatest commandment in all of the world?" Jesus replied:

> "You shall love the Lord your God with all your heart, with all your soul, and with all your mind. This is the great and first commandment. And a second is like it, You shall love your neighbor as yourself" (Matt. 22:37–39).

Jesus knew that if you don't love yourself, it is impossible to love other people. Those who dislike themselves will have a tough time building a relationship with others.

THE "BEAUTY CULT" BECKONS

Modern-day society doesn't help matters much. Our society has put forth some false standards of what it means to be "good" or "beautiful." This "beauty cult" encourages the false notion that to be worth something, you must be beautiful. The sad fact is—we buy into it! We all want to look good, have good posture, smell good, dress well. Supposedly, one of the highest compliments we can be paid is to be told we are beautiful or handsome. But God doesn't love us or accept us simply because of our looks. God loves us with an uncompromising, unconditional, beautiful love that only can be explained in God's terms.

We also find ourselves playing the "intelligence game," thinking that our self-worth hinges on whether or not we are intelligent. We want to be knowledgeable and witty, and we want our children to be "exceptional" children. We would like to see them begin walking and talking at an early age, and we feel a certain pride when our children are placed in advanced programs in their schools. But there is a danger in believing that a higher IQ places a higher value on a person in God's eyes. It does not. God doesn't love anyone more or less, simply because of their grade point average. He accepts us with our successes and failures. God doesn't judge us by our brains.

Too, the "moneybags game" can lead us to believe that the higher our monetary worth, the higher our spiritual worth. We become caught up in acquiring status symbols—fine homes, nice cars, fashionable clothes. But these very symbols of status can turn into dangerous obstacles to our spiritual growth and development. We tend to place value on the material possessions surrounding us, not realizing that God's opinion of us and His love for us have nothing to do with our materialism. God's love transcends all money, power, materialism, intelligence, or beauty—or the lack thereof!

Thus, we have every reason to have a positive self-image. If Christ loves us unconditionally, we can love ourselves unconditionally. Self-image is simply what we think of ourselves. It is the mental picture we have painted of ourselves. Throughout our lives, all of us have painted on the canvas of our minds the picture of the person we think we are. The Bible underscores this by saying:

As [a man] thinketh in his heart, so is he (Prov. 23:7).

You have an image of yourself. If that image is poor, it will be difficult for you to raise your commitment to God or your personal standards of living until you raise that self-image.

HIDING THE PROBLEM

One of the surest signs of a bad self-image is *withdrawal*. People who feel inferior tend to withdraw socially and emotionally, often into silence and loneliness. They think, "Why try anymore? I'm a failure." Many people allow feelings of inferiority and failure to follow them throughout life, even to their graves.

Another sign of a poor self-image is a *false aggressiveness*. Some people have personalities that seem to come on a little too strongly. They tend to carry a chip on their shoulder as if to say, "The world owes me!" They lash out at others and are quick-tempered and hostile. Their attitude says clearly, "I'm going to 'get' other people before other people 'get' me. I'm going to do them in first! This world is trying to take advantage of me, and I don't like it."

Others with self-image problems express an *uncomfortable kind of humor*. These people want to feel accepted, but feel that their lives are not completely up to par. So, they laugh at themselves and make jokes about themselves as if to say, "I've accepted my weaknesses and can laugh about them." But what they really mean is, "I've not been able to accept this flaw in my life. But if I laugh and joke about it, maybe you will think I've grown to the point where I have been able to accept it." When these people are alone, however, they are unable to shake the deep sense of depression that sets in when they don't feel accepted.

Still others have such poor self-images that they try to *deny reality* all together. These are the people who are most susceptible to drug addiction and alcoholism. There are more than nine million alcoholics in America today, and a majority of them are in that situation because of poor self-images. They were unhappy with themselves and with their lives, so they tried to find something that would enable them to deny reality and the accompanying experiences and pressures of life. Some drink themselves into oblivion—a severe denial of reality.

Conformity is another way some people deal with poor self-images. They fear being different and abhor the possibility of rejection. They have no idea who they really are because they have patterned their lives after other people. Therefore, they walk, talk, and dress like other people. They fear just being themselves and find it difficult to accept honest and helpful criticism. They can't laugh at themselves, and their "I don't care" attitude leaves them with very few friends.

We need to recognize that God wants us to have good self-images. He wants us to have a good feeling about who and what we are. Our self-image is important because our behavior reflects our image of ourselves. Just by observing how we behave, others can tell what we think of ourselves.

A positive self-image can determine how successful we are in life. So many people have such tremendous potential, yet they go through life missing that potential because of poor self-images. Our self-concept is the core of our personality. Self-image affects every aspect of human behavior—the ability to learn, the capacity to grow and change, and the choice of friends, mates, and careers. It is no exaggeration that a strong positive self-image is the best possible preparation for success in life.

THE GREATEST CHRISTIAN IN THE WORLD

There are many people who feel that they do not deserve success. When they develop their careers, they will grow to the point of almost achieving success, but will fall backward at the last minute because they don't feel they truly deserve to reach that highest peak. Many Christians fall into that same trap. Most Christians picture themselves as struggling to live the Christian life—struggling with Satan, struggling with temptation—and falling flat on their faces. So much of what is preached today as biblical standards of Christian living actually is a contradiction to what the Word of God truly teaches. It is so important that we visualize ourselves as growing to become the greatest Christians who ever lived.

I have a personal goal to be the greatest Christian that the world ever has known, other than Jesus Christ. You might think that I am an egotistical braggart, but it doesn't matter. I may not achieve that goal, but nevertheless, it should be the standard that guides my life. My goal should not be to be like any other Christian. I need to strive to be like Christ—the only perfect standard for my life. As I understand the Scripture, my goal as a Christian should be to strive for perfection. Unless I really believe that, I don't think there is any possibility of achieving any of the qualities of Christ in my life.

Self-image determines our productivity for God. Ephesians 1:5 says:

> He destined us in love to be his sons through Jesus Christ, according to the purpose of his will.

God intends for us to know that we are His children, and as heirs of God we have access to all that God is. That should motivate us to strive high and be pleased with ourselves. For it is not our humanity that gives us worth, but our relationship to God our Father.

WALKING THE PLANK

The mind has a way of completing whatever picture we put into it, so it is important to make sure our self-image is a good one. Each of us lives in accordance with the picture in his "mental computer." If you think of yourself as a phony, you will live like a phony. If you think of yourself as a committed Christian, you will live like a committed Christian.

To test this fact, take a plank twelve inches wide and place it on the ground. Now, walk across that plank from end to end. No problem. Next, take that same plank and raise it twenty feet above the ground. Stand at the end of the plank and walk across it again. The thought of walking across that plank, now elevated high above the ground, makes most of us frightened. Something happened inside of us because we mentally pictured falling off that board.

Many people walked by a large slab of marble and said, "That's just an old, ugly chunk of stone." But Michelangelo saw the same piece of marble and said, "There's a statue of Moses in that marble." Once he saw it, he was able to fashion it into a likeness of his mental picture. The same principle holds true in life. If you can't see God doing something great in you, you will never be able to make anything significant or valuable out of your life.

Our sinful nature is the worst enemy of a good self-image because sin creates guilt, and guilt creates a sense of failure and uselessness. As we repeatedly sin, guilt grinds away at us, slowly destroying our conscience. Often, we don't realize what is happening until we are emotionally drained or destroyed.

Developing a good self-image begins with giving your heart to Christ and accepting God's forgiveness. Salvation is the first step in solving almost any problem you might have, and without a doubt, it is the first step in overcoming a self-image problem. Romans 5:8 says:

While we were yet sinners Christ died for us.

Jesus' death on the cross affirms two basic revelations— we needed Jesus to die for us because we are sinners, and we were worthy of His death on the cross. Jesus died because we needed it and because we are of value. Even if you were the only person who ever sinned against God, you are of such significant worth and value that our Lord would have died for you alone.

You will never have a good self-image until your relationship with God is right through Jesus Christ. Accept Him as your personal Lord and Savior. It is also important to accept God's total forgiveness of your sins. Our God is a forgiving God.

He forgives us for our past sins, for our present sins, and for our future sins. It is important to accept that forgiveness and to gratefully acknowledge His unconditional love.

NO NEED TO BARGAIN

There is no need to bargain with God. Some people, even well-intentioned Christians, will try to work hard as if to have something to swap for God's love, acceptance, and approval.

Instead of bargaining, *become involved with God in the dynamic purpose of glorifying Him.* One of the best ways to raise our self-esteem is to feel that we are helping or assisting God in making this a better world in which to live. For this reason, undergirding a church is so important, because we link hands and lives with other people—not perfect people, but people who are willing to look beyond their own selfishness to make this world a better place.

Become willing to share yourself with others, as you have shared yourself with God. Sharing has a way of drawing us out as we share our faith, our time and our possessions. Don't be afraid to open your life to others.

Finally, *saturate yourself with Scripture.* The Word of God is a Book written to tell us about God's plan for our lives. It is not a "no-no" Book, and it was not written to make us feel like heels. Rather, the Bible was written to reveal God's wonderful love for us. As you consistently read from His Word, you will begin to see how much God does love you. When you see how much God loves you, you will begin to love yourself as much as He does.

As you begin to lift your self-image, take comfort and encouragement from the following revised version of 1 Corinthians 13 by Dick Dickenson:

Because God loves me, he is slow to lose patience with me.
Because God loves me, he takes the circumstances of my life
and uses them in a constructive way for my growth.

Because God loves me, he does not treat me as an object to be possessed and manipulated.

Because God loves me, he has no need to impress me with how great and powerful he is, because he is God.

Nor does he belittle me as his child in order to show me how important he is.

Because God loves me, he is for me. He wants to see me mature and develop in his love.

Because God loves me, he does not send down his wrath on every little mistake I make, of which there are many.

Because God loves me, he does not keep score of all my sins and beat me over the head with them whenever he gets the chance.

Because God loves me, he is deeply grieved if I do not walk in the ways that please him, because he sees that this is evidence that I don't trust him and love him as I should.

Because God loves me, he rejoices when I experience his power and strength and stand up under the pressures of life for his name sake.

Because God loves me, he keeps on working patiently with me, even when I feel like giving up and can't see why he doesn't give up with me, too.

Because God loves me, he keeps on trusting me, when at times I don't even trust myself.

Because God loves me, he never says there is no hope for me, but rather he patiently works with me, loves me, and disciples me in such a way that it is hard for me to understand the depth of his concern for me.

Because God loves me, he never forsakes me, even though many of my friends might.

Because God loves me, he stands with me when I have reached the rock bottom of despair.

When I see the real me and compare that with his righteousness, beauty, and love—it is at a moment like this that I can really believe that God loves me.

Yes, the greatest of all gifts is God's perfect love.[2]

CONQUERING FRUSTRATION

The worst things:
To be in bed and sleep not,
To want for one who comes not,
To try to please and please not.

— Egyptian proverb

6

Elijah, one of the great men of the Bible, once became so overwhelmingly frustrated that he begged God to take his life. We learn the reason for his desperation in 1 Kings 19:

Ahab told Jezebel all that Elijah had done, and how he had slain all the prophets with the sword. Then Jezebel sent a messenger to Elijah, saying, "So may the gods do to me, and more also, if I do not make your life as the life of one of them by this time tomorrow." Then he was afraid, and he arose and went for his life, and came to Beer-sheba, which belongs to Judah, and left his servant there.

But he himself went a day's journey into the wilderness, and came and sat down under a broom tree; and he asked that he might die, saying, "It is enough; now, O LORD, take away my life; for I am no better than my fathers." And he lay down and slept under a broom tree; and behold, an angel touched him, and said to him, "Arise and eat." . . .

He said, "I have been very jealous for the LORD, the God of hosts; for the people of Israel have forsaken thy covenant, thrown down thy altars, and slain thy prophets with the sword; and I, even I only, am left; and they seek my life, to take it away" (vv. 1–5, 10).

Maybe Elijah should have read Psalms 37:1:

Fret not yourself because of the wicked.

In other words, don't allow yourself to become frustrated because of the evil actions or misbehavior of other people. The psalmist continued:

Be not envious of wrongdoers! For they will soon fade like the grass, and wither like the green herb. Trust in the LORD, and do good; so you will dwell in the land, and enjoy security. Take delight in the LORD, and he will give you the desires of your heart. Commit your way to the LORD; trust in him, and he will act (vv. 1–5).

You might not be quite as desperate as Elijah was, but there's a good chance that some sort of frustration is robbing you of inner peace.

Some years ago, a popular song called "Don't Fence Me In" carried the lyrical phrase, "Give a man a horse he can ride, where there are no fences to stop him." [1] In the background could be heard the clippity clop of horses' hooves. The song implied that to be happy, you need to be free to roam where there are no fences, barriers, or obstacles—only limitless prairies.

Life is *not* a limitless prairie. It is full of challenges, barriers, fences, and canyons. It is impossible to live life without experiencing some difficulties, problems, and frustrations, no matter whether you are a non-believer or a dedicated Christian. Regardless of your circumstances in life, there will always be frustrations of one sort or another within the home, on the job, among friends and relatives, and even within the church.

However, we have been given a guidebook to deal with any frustration we might encounter—the Bible. Not only does Scripture contain the message of Christian faith and the hope of eternal life with God in heaven, but it also offers practical guidelines for dealing with any problem we might face here on earth. Through God's Word we discover that Jesus Christ can live within us, sustaining us and giving us wisdom to deal with annoying and frustrating situations in our lives. Life is full of frustrations, but I am convinced that the Christian perspective—the Christian frame of reference—is the only way to successfully deal with them and learn from them.

DEAD-END STREETS AND HUMAN 'MACHINES'

Frustration simply means "in vain." It means to try and try, but to be unsuccessful in the attempt. It means to be thwarted by fences we cannot get through or go over—to be blocked by circumstances in our lives that we seem unable to change. Frustration can be wanting something that you cannot have, or striving for something that always eludes you. You feel as if you are blundering down a dead-end street, going down a blind alley, getting nowhere for all of your trying. Frustration can turn into an emotional preoccupation that feeds upon itself until, in the end, you can't remember what you were frustrated about to begin with!

Our *complicated society* is one of the chief causes of frustration. Work used to be a simple, predictable factor in the growth of the nation. For many of our parents or grandparents, work meant getting up every morning at five o'clock, going out to milk the cow, tend to the farm animals, till and plant the fields, cook and clean and repair—and then coming in at twilight, physically exhausted. The work was hard, but it was simple, not encumbered by modern technological advances that often can confuse us and upset our emotional well-being. And at the end of the day, there was something to show for all that hard work.

Today, the vast majority of people are frustrated because they feel they have been turned into "machines" that have to be turned on at eight and then turned off at five. Just flip the switch! As one writer lamented:

I work, work, work without end.
Why and for whom, I know not.
I care not. I ask not.
I am a machine.[2]

In the modern-day age, there is a prevalent sense of desperation about the *future of our society* that also is creating a
deep sense of frustration. Many people hold jobs that are so
tightly connected to the economic health of the nation that
the slightest fluctuation can either cause great despair or bring
needed financial relief. But the economic uncertainty is unnerv-
ing, particularly for those in sales positions or other jobs where
there is no steady income. For them, frustration has become
a way of life.

Robert E. Lee once was asked the best route from Lexington,
Virginia, to another city. He answered, "It makes little difference, for whatever route you select, you will wish you had
taken the other." Those experiencing financial frustrations can
relate to Lee's profound reply. No matter what decision is
made about a job or financial matter, there's a strong feeling
that another decision would have been better. The uncertainty
about the future weighs heavily upon them, and they often
feel there is nowhere to turn.

Physical problems, too, can cause frustration. People troubled with rheumatism, migraine headaches, arthritis, weak
backs, or numerous other ailments cannot accomplish some
of the things they want to because of physical limitations. A
lingering sense of frustration easily sets in.

Bad habits can create frustration, especially when the habit
has become addictive to the point that you feel unable to shake
it or control it. It is controlling you, and you feel defeated,
overcome by it. Some bad habits—alcoholism, all sorts of drug
abuse, patterns of violence—can be so destructive that they
threaten to shorten your life and damage your relationships
with your family and friends.

Competition to succeed is another frustration-causing factor
in our society. The success syndrome says, "I've got to have

as much as they have, if not more." The pressure to be success-ful, to collect material possessions, is so strong that many be-come obsessed by the effort. We never can obtain everything we want, so we become frustrated. And the harder we try to get more, more, more the more frustrated we become.

LIKE A FLY IN A TRAP

When I think of frustration, I most often think of a tiny fly trapped inside a car, trying desperately to get out. It buzzes around inside, then darts repeatedly toward freedom, only to be knocked down time and time again by the clear, raised windowpanes. That little fly reminds me of a lot of people who have no inner resource of a meaningful faith to draw from during times of frustration. They keep "hitting the glass," continually being thwarted, not making any progress.

Frustration affects everyone, and it is a "kill-joy" that tran-scends time. The Bible gives a variety of examples of people who experienced frustration. We've already seen how deep frustration drove Elijah to the point that he wanted God to take his life. When God wanted Moses to speak to a rock in order to draw forth water, Moses succumbed to frustration and struck the rock instead. Martha grew frustrated with Mary for talking with Jesus in another room instead of helping her prepare the evening meal. The disciples became anxious and frustrated one day when lunchtime rolled around and there was not enough food to feed the thousands of people gathered to hear Jesus speak. On another occasion, some disciples brought a man to be healed by Jesus, but the crowd was so thick they couldn't get near. Frustrated, they finally tore off the roof and lowered the man to Jesus through the ceiling.

When we encounter frustrations, there can be either positive or negative results. On the negative side, we can allow frustra-tion to render us unable to accomplish anything of value when we do not deal with the problem responsibly. Frustration al-lowed to rule unchecked in our lives can destroy friendships—

and even self-confidence. When we become uptight and frustrated, our witness for Christ is ineffective. It becomes difficult to convince others that Jesus Christ can change their lives when we Christians refuse to allow Him to soothe the frustrations in our own lives. Frustration also can damage our health, when we allow stress, tension, frustration and pressure to eat away inside. Refusing to deal responsibly with frustration literally can take years off our lives.

At the other end of the spectrum are positive results. Frustration can challenge our creativity and personal initiative when circumstances seem unbearably difficult and insurmountable. The biographies of many great people testify to the power of the inner spirit to overcome barriers.

Demosthenes, the Athenian orator and statesman, was once a stutterer. To overcome that handicap, he went to the roaring sea, placed pebbles in his mouth, and talked to the ocean. Eventually, he overcame his speech problem and became an eloquent orator.

American clergyman and lecturer Henry Ward Beecher was once a shy, clumsy boy, his speech blurred by an enlarged palate. But with the help of God, he developed poise and power in his speech, affecting thousands with his messages.

The great writer Robert Louis Stevenson became an invalid, but he refused to give in to frustration. He wrote many beloved stories while confined to his bed.

The renowned inventor Thomas Edison blundered into one obstacle after another on his way to developing the electric light bulb. One night, his friend Cloyd Chapman walked in and found Edison smiling smugly in his laboratory. "Have you solved it?" he asked Edison. Edison responded, "Not a blamed thing works, but now I can start all over again." He had refused to let frustration prevent him from achieving.

But perhaps the greatest testimony to overcoming frustration is the story of Jesus facing the crucifixion. Everything seemed to be going against Christ. He was captured, beaten, tortured, blasphemed, and spat upon. Finally, His torturers hung Him on the cross to die. But what seemed to be the greatest defeat in history was turned into the greatest victory. Not only did Christ provide forgiveness and redemption for our sins, but He made it possible for us to become the people that God wants us to be. Through Jesus, we have access to the grace and strength of God to help us rule victoriously over any problem we may encounter.

WE'RE ONLY HUMAN

To overcome frustration, you must first *be honest with yourself* and accept the fact that you are a weak and frail human, vulnerable to frustrations. The apostle Paul warned that no one should "think of himself more highly than he ought to think" (Rom. 12:3). We need to recognize that we can't do everything. We should use our God-given talents and abilities to their fullest but still realize that there are some things God simply doesn't need or want us to achieve. So we ought not become frustrated when everything we plan or attempt doesn't turn out just right.

Second, *accept the talents and abilities of other people.* There will be some people who can achieve in areas in which you cannot achieve. They may have certain skills you do not have. But that doesn't mean they are more important than you in God's sight. Don't be jealous or envious of their talents. Concentrate on your own abilities and find ways to maximize them for God's glory.

Third, *acknowledge the presence of God's power within you.* There are a lot of circumstances of life that we as mere human beings cannot change. But we can concentrate on developing the inner strength necessary to handle frustrations. Through our faith, Jesus Christ can participate with us in dealing with our problems and frustrations. When we say "Emmanuel," we are recognizing that God is with us, He is in us, and He is here helping us cope with life.

Luke 17:21 says:

The kingdom of God is within you (KJV).

Colossians 3:15 tells us:

And let the peace of Christ rule in your hearts, to which indeed you were called in the one body.

Isaiah 30:15 advises us:

In quietness and in trust shall be your strength.

John 14:27 gives us this promise from God:

Peace I leave with you; my peace I give to you; not as the world gives do I give to you. Let not your hearts be troubled, neither let them be afraid.

When frustrations come we need to pray: *God, I know You are interested in me and that You are aware of the situation. I know that You are inside of me, and I am depending upon You to give me some strength to deal with this situation.* By so doing, you will be practicing the presence of Jesus, becoming consciously aware that Jesus Christ is with us to help us.

We can benefit, too, by the advice a pastor once gave a church member. The man was frustrated to the point that he was continually tense and nervous. The pastor had the man recline in a lounge chair and shut his eyes. Next, he told him to picture Jesus standing right beside him, ministering to him. The pastor encouraged the man to talk with God, saying, "Jesus, I love You. Jesus, put Your hand on my shoulder and calm me down. I need Your strength in my life." The pastor went through an entire prayer, asking his friend to visually think about Christ beside him throughout the entire time. After he finished, the man reported that the experience had been one of the most meaningful times of prayer that he had ever had. This is but one way to practice the presence of Jesus.

Additionally, work on overcoming frustration by living one

day at a time. Too many people are frustrated because they are dwelling on what happened yesterday, or they are worried about what will happen tomorrow. We all could benefit from this advice from Alcoholics Anonymous:

Just for Today

Just for today, I will live through the next twelve hours
and not tackle my whole life's problems at once.
Just for today, I will improve my mind.
I will learn something useful.
I will read something that requires effort,
thought and concentration.
Just for today, I will be agreeable.
I will look my best,
speak in a well-modulated voice,
be courteous and considerate.
Just for today, I will not find fault
with friend, relative or colleague.
I won't try to change or improve anyone
but myself.
Just for today, I will have a program.
I might not follow it exactly, but I will have it.
I will save myself from two enemies: hurry and indecision.
Just for today, I will exercise my character in three ways.
I will do a good turn and keep it secret.
If anyone finds out, it won't count.
Just for today, I will do two things I don't want to do,
just for exercise.
Just for today, I will be unafraid.
Especially will I be unafraid to enjoy what is beautiful
and believe that as I give to the world,
the world will give to me,
living one day at a time.*

God wants to help us through every crisis and problem we encounter. The message of Jesus Christ is one of forgiveness,

---

* From *Twenty-Four Hours a Day,* Hazeldon, copyright 1975, by Hazeldon Foundation, Center City, MN. Reprinted by permission.

of promise of the life to come. It is a practical message for today as we try to overcome frustrations in life. Those with a meaningful faith in Jesus Christ are better able to cope with all of the frustrations and conflicts inherent in living. If you have never made that discovery of Jesus Christ as your personal Savior, I invite and challenge you to accept Him today!

CONQUERING
MEDIOCRITY

We seldom break our leg
so long as life continues
a toilsome upward climb.
The danger comes when
we begin to take things easily
and choose the convenient paths.

– Friedrich Nietzsche
*Miscellaneous Maxims
and Opinions*

7

God loves us so very much that He wants to accomplish His best in and through our lives. Yet, sadly, less than 5 percent of the people today are achieving their full potential, the kind of potential God wants for their lives. There is so much mediocrity in most people's lives that it can't help but disturb and break the heart of our Creator. There is no doubt that God wants us to accomplish something significant with our lives.

The plans of the mind belong to man, but the answer of the tongue is from the LORD. All the ways of a man are pure in his own eyes, but the LORD weighs the spirit. Commit your work to the Lord, and your plans will be established. The LORD has made everything for its purpose, even the wicked for the day of trouble. Every one who is arrogant is an abomination to the LORD; be assured, he will not go unpunished. By loyalty and faithfulness iniquity is atoned for, and by the fear of the LORD a man avoids evil. When a man's ways please the LORD, he makes even his enemies to be at peace with him. Better is a little with righteousness than great revenues with injustice. A man's mind plans his way, but the LORD directs his steps (Prov. 16:1–9).

The world is packed full of people who are settling for less than the best in their lives. Whether in school, business, family, church, or community relationships, too many people are content with less than they should. In plain terms, many of them are downright lazy, leading undisciplined lives which prevent them from reaching the highest levels of achievement which God would like to see them achieve. After all, God made us, and He knows best what we ought to achieve in our lives.

Examine your own life. Are you getting what you really want most in life? Do you feel as if you are losing control of your own destiny? Do you find yourself surrendering the leadership of your life to runaway emotions and "down" moods? Do you truly have a desire for worthwhile achievements? Do you desire to get a grip on your anger and be able to master your moods? Do you long to succeed in areas of your life where you have previously failed? If so, there is only one way to conquer mediocrity: through self-discipline.

Without self-discipline, we eat too much, become morally weak and intellectually dull, stop expanding our horizons, become enslaved to harmful habits, allow bad moods to master us, spend too much money—the list goes on. Without self-discipline, we are overrun by negative emotions that can give rise to destructive behavior, creating havoc in our relationships with others. But more importantly, without self-discipline, we fail to achieve God's highest dreams and ambitions for our lives.

NO WALLFLOWERS, PLEASE

Let me challenge you to do something great with your life. Do you want to be in that 95 percent of folks who are failing to achieve their potential? Or do you want to reach the heights of achievement? God did not put you on this planet to be a wallflower. We are all to make positive contributions, helping God to make this a better world.

You will never reach that full potential, however, unless you determine to become a disciplined person. There is something about human nature that resists discipline. There is a natural inclination in all of us to "go off." If we continually did as we pleased, most of the time we would be doing nothing. Call it the lazy man's religion, if you please. Proverbs 13:4 says:

> Lazy people want much, but get little while the diligent are prospering (TLB).

If you are inclined to laziness, ask God to give you the desire and the strength to settle for nothing less than achieving your full potential. As long as you have a streak of laziness, you never will achieve anything worthwhile with your life.

Many people do not understand self-discipline. Self-discipline is not a dirty word. It is a positive word that signifies the means to reach your goals. It is a way to improve yourself, to help you make the right choices between better and best. It is the arrow that keeps you on target. Contrary to popular thought, self-discipline does not merely mean restraint, but rather is a preparation for release. It is not a loss of freedom but is the road to greater freedom. It is not holding back but moving forward . . . not an enemy but a friend . . . not self-punishment but self-control . . . not a slave but a master. Self-discipline is not an end unto itself, but is the beginning and the path to all worthwhile achievements.

No one ever has been able to make a significant contribution to our world without the principles of self-discipline. As 1 Corinthians 9:25 says:

> To win the contest, you must deny yourself many things that would keep you from doing your best (TLB).

The only way to overcome mediocrity and become an achiever is to practice self-discipline in your life. It will make your mind sharper and quicker, bring more energy and zest to keep you going, and provide the capacity to keep you cool when others are losing their tempers. Self-discipline will make you feel like a champ, instead of a chump.

THE WORLD'S GREATEST

In the 1976 Montreal Olympics, twenty-six-year-old Bruce Jenner won a grueling ten-day decathlon. He was acclaimed the world's greatest athlete. How did he do it? Did he say, "Well, maybe one of these days, if I get around to it, I'll become the world's greatest athlete"? Not on your life! He set that as his goal, and he was willing to discipline himself so that he could develop and attain it. He trained long and hard, seven hours a day for four years. Self-discipline made it possible to achieve that tremendous goal.

How do you become a more self-disciplined person? How do you become such an achiever? One way is to recognize your need for self-discipline. Without that recognition, you never can begin the process. Just like the "Do Not Disturb" signs on hotel room doors, many people wear invisible signs that say they want to be left alone, undisturbed, unchanged. As long as you have the attitude that you are content with your life the way it is, you will never be able to grow and expand your faith, your way of life, or any achievement in your life. You must be willing to see the need in your life for self-discipline before you will be able to grow.

There are no shortcuts to self-discipline. In fact, there are no shortcuts to doing anything great or significant with your life. There is an old English proverb that says, "He who would climb the ladder must begin at the bottom." Too often we want achievement or success without making any personal investment. You can't automatically jump to the top. It takes discipline to make the long hard climb, hand over hand, rung over rung. But the end result is well worth the effort.

You can find the motivation to become self-disciplined

through a *personal encounter with Jesus Christ.* Christianity is not just a ticket to heaven when we die—it is a way of life *now.* Jesus Christ can give you an added dimension to your life. He can determine your way of thinking, your way of behavior. When people invite Jesus Christ into their lives, they experience God's love and presence, and they receive access to God's power in their lives. He gives us plans for our lives and then provides the resources to carry out those plans. You never can become a truly self-disciplined person in the highest sense of the word without a personal relationship with Jesus Christ. He doesn't make you less of a person, He makes you *more* of a person. No matter how good your life is, Jesus Christ can enter into every dimension of your life and make it better.

The next step in becoming a self-disciplined person is to *begin disciplining yourself in all the little areas of your life.* Sometimes, those little areas can make the biggest differences. It might be that you need to discipline yourself to keep a clean car, or a clean room, or school locker, or desktop. Or perhaps you need to discipline yourself to make better use of your time. To become disciplined in the large areas of your life, you must first be willing to begin with the small areas.

I DARE YOU!

As a child, William Danforth was very anemic and frail. When his family moved from the city to the country, he found his classmates to be much healthier than he was. One day, his teacher challenged him to become the healthiest boy in his class. In his book, *I Dare You,* Danforth recalled her challenge: "I dare you to fill your body with fresh air, pure water, wholesome food, and daily exercise until your cheeks are rosy, your chest full, and your limbs sturdy." As he heard that dare, something within Danforth began to surge with strength, enthusiasm, and power. He set as his goal to do exactly that, to become the healthiest boy in his class—and he did! Danforth later became the founder of Ralston Purina and a very successful businessman. A friend later described him as giving the best that was in him, "whether he was guiding a great industry, traveling in a remote corner of the world, shooting ducks, or playing with his grandchildren. The day ahead was always the most thrilling day of his life. The job at hand was always the most important one he ever had undertaken. He never gave less than his best. He was truly a self-disciplined man." [1]

You, too, can dare to believe that you can achieve God's best and highest in your life. One reason the Christian faith is so important is because it teaches us to believe. If you can develop a meaningful faith and truly believe in God through Jesus Christ, you can have that principle and power of belief that will affect every other area of your life. John 20:31 says:

> But these are written, that ye might believe that Jesus is the Christ, the Son of God; and that believing ye might have life through his name (KJV).

The word "belief" appears ninety-eight times in the Gospel of John. That same word can transform the impossible into the possible.

Why do we have churches? In simple terms, it is because groups of people are willing to believe that God wants to do something significant in and through their lives. They come week by week to be a part of this church—to participate in this believing attitude—believing that God will work significantly in their lives. God wants to do amazing things with us if we will just give Him the opportunity.

If you believe you can do something, obstacles can never make you give up. If you believe you cannot do something, you will be more inclined to give up at the first sign of trouble. How is the faith factor in your life? Dare to believe that you can achieve God's best and highest in your life!

But don't stop there. Dream a lofty dream. Imagination is a tremendous gift from God. It is the ability to think about something you have never seen or experienced. Every great invention is the product of someone's dream. Someone dreamed it, conceived it, thought it through, and it became a reality. Proverbs 29:18 says:

Where there is no vision, the people perish (KJV).

Everyone needs a dream. It will make you bounce out of bed in the morning. It will heighten your senses and make your creative juices flow. It will lift you up and put zest in your daily living. Dreams are God-given to help you set and reach great goals.

A CLASSROOM EXPERIMENT

A teacher once had her class conduct an experiment with "jumping fleas." The students put hundreds of the fleas on a table and observed how high they jumped. Then they took a large glass container and turned it upside down over the jumping fleas. Now when they jumped, they kept hitting the top of the container until they finally realized they couldn't go any higher. The teacher later removed the container, but the fleas continued to jump to the same height, as if the container were still overhead. They had restrained their ability to jump to only what they thought was their limit.

The same is true with many people's minds today. They have put a lid on their minds and refuse to believe that they can jump higher and higher, achieving something greater with their lives. Consequently, mediocrity sets in. This is especially true in terms of spiritual faith when people cannot imagine themselves being more committed, more dedicated, or possessing any more faith for spiritual commitment.

For centuries, men dreamed of running the four-minute mile. But it was not until 1954, when a medical doctor expanded his mind and believed that he could accomplish that goal, that it was done. His accomplishment seemed to break the mental barriers in a lot of other people. In the following years, hundreds of people began to do the same thing! He simply expanded their thinking.

What beautiful dreams do you have in *your* life? Would you like to see them fulfilled in your lifetime? Andrew Carnegie once said, "All achievements—all earned riches—had their beginnings in an idea."

But the average person today has no objectives or goals. Most people do not know how to answer the question, "What would you like to do with your life?" They simply do not know what they want. It is vitally important to decide what you want to do and who you want to be, so that you do not just drift through life. Instead, go after the best things in life. Matthew 6:19–21 tells us:

> Lay not up for yourselves treasures upon earth, where moth and rust doth corrupt and where thieves break through and steal: But lay up for yourselves treasures in heaven, where neither moth nor rust doth corrupt, and where thieves do not break through nor steal: For where your treasure is, there will your heart be also.

True success begins by putting God first in your life, followed by your family relationships, and then your relationships with others. And to truly do something great with your life, remember that there will be some sacrifices involved. You must be willing to forfeit some things so that something better can come along.

DON'T GIVE UP

In 1968 Rocky Bleier was the eighteenth pick of the Pittsburgh Steelers, but before he had an opportunity to play, he was sent to Vietnam for nine months. While there, one of his feet was crippled by an exploding grenade. One shoe was half the size of the other because of the serious injury. When he returned home, he was told that he would never play professional football. But Bleier refused to accept that gloomy prediction. Every day, he put himself through excruciating and agonizing pain, disciplining his body back into shape. Finally, he was able to run faster than ever before because of his dedicated self-discipline. The nation watched as this young man made a tremendous contribution to the Steelers team. He had been willing to pay the price!

Many people have good intentions. They will start achieving their goals, but will allow failures, obstacles, misunderstandings, heartaches, and other problems to stand in the way of success. They just give up.

You never will make a contribution to this world if you throw up your hands and quit when the going gets rough. Don't give up the struggle if it is something good, if it brings honor to God, or if it is something that would please our Lord. You will be blessed for overcoming whatever obstacle might stand in your way, and for pressing on.

. . . press on toward the goal for the prize of the upward call of God in Christ Jesus (Phil. 3:14).

CONQUERING POOR VALUES

Character cannot be
developed in ease and quiet:
Only through experience of trial and
suffering can the soul be strengthened,
vision cleared, ambition inspired,
and success achieved.

– Helen Keller
Helen Keller's Journal

8

Define character.

That's a tough one, isn't it? It's a hard trait to define, yet one that is so vital to success in any aspect of life.

Let's examine the word "character" in the biblical sense. Our world is desperately in need of men and women who have developed a depth of character, and there is no better place to study how than through God's Word.

In 2 Peter 1:5-7 we are instructed to:

> . . . make every effort to supplement your faith with virtue, and virtue with knowledge, and knowledge with self-control, and self-control with steadfastness, and steadfastness with godliness, and godliness with brotherly affection, and brotherly affection with love.

During the Korean War, some fine American soldiers underwent an extreme crisis in their lives when they were captured by the enemy. They turned their backs on their country, even their friends. Studies have been conducted to determine what

happened. The conclusion? These men experienced a break-
down in character. One U.S. Army official said, "By the time
a young man enters the Army, he should possess a set of
moral values, and the strength of character to live by them."
Yet, how many of us would have failed that test of character?

Character has been defined as "the ability to determine right
from wrong and then force the self to choose the right." The
Bible has much to say about developing that ability to discern
right from wrong. Our inner development will dictate the way
we behave, and that is why Jesus concentrated on teaching
us to give priority to what we do with our life. If we are the
types of people God wants us to be on the inside—our inner
core—then our behavior will fit that pattern. But we often
live irresponsibly because we have a poor set of values and
are missing something vital on the inside. Let's explore that
mystical "inner something" that is so vital to conquering poor
values and developing a Christian character.

When Christ comes into a life, He transforms it and begins
the process of character development. A significant and wonderful change becomes evident in our thinking and in our behavior as we allow Him to mold our values.

Why should we seek a depth of character? One prime reason
is because one day *we will be judged by our character.* In 2
Corinthians 5:10 Paul tells us:

> For we must all appear before the judgment seat of Christ, so
> that each one may receive good or evil, according to what he
> has done in the body.

But even though we know about that final day of judgment
when our character will be evaluated, most of us still proceed
through life uncommitted to character development. We know
about it, but don't put that knowledge into practice.

A salesman once tried to sell a farmer a magazine, telling
him that the magazine would show how he could improve
his farming methods by 50 percent. The farmer wasn't the
least bit interested. "Why not?" asked the salesman. "I already

know how to farm 100 percent better than I am farming now," was the farmer's reply. That's the way it is with most of us right now. We already know more than we are applying in our daily lives. We don't suffer from a lack of information. We suffer for not applying what we know to our day-to-day living. But one day we will pay the consequences when we stand before God, judged on our character. How will you stand the test?

Another reason we need to conquer poor values and develop character is because *our eternal life is affected by what we do in this life.* One fable tells of a wealthy man who asked his contractor son to build a fine home for a special client. Money was no object. In fact, the father gave his son an enormous sum up front to spend on the home, emphasizing again how the son was to spare no cost to build an exquisite mansion. Instead, the son squandered most of the money and ended up having to cut corners by using cheaper building materials. "It won't make any difference," the son thought to himself. "No one will know. The home looks fine on the outside. They won't be able to tell that I've trimmed down the quality." To the son's surprise, his father turned over the keys and the title to that house to him! He was that "special client," and didn't even know it.

That's the kind of life too many of us are building today—cutting corners, trimming back on quality, making inferior decisions. One day we, too, will find that we will reap our eternal rewards based on the lives we lead today. Remember 2 Corinthians 5:10? ". . . each one may receive good or evil, according to what he has done in the body." The Bible clearly states that our heavenly reward will be based on our earthly lives.

But heavenly rewards aside, there is another reason that we should strive to build a Christian character—because of *our influence on others.* That influence will linger on long after we die. How are you thought of now, and how will you be remembered? Good or bad, your sphere of influence will not die with you. Wolfgang Mozart died at age thirty-five, but his music lives on today. Italian Renaissance painter and architect Raphael died at age thirty-seven, but his art lives on and is appreciated today. Your life, your influence will continue to impact the lives of those who survive you—whether that influence is good or bad.

Finally, and just as importantly, Christians should seek to develop a Christian character to *grow in the likeness and image of God.* Just as a child grows as part of the natural maturing process, so should Christians mature as we strive for a Christlike, spiritual state of heart and mind and life.

CHARACTER BUILDING

Now back to 2 Peter. There is some powerful advice for us as we begin the pilgrimage to develop a solid, Christian character. The first quality mentioned in that passage is *virtue,* or goodness. Is it possible to be "good" without being "goody-goody"? Without a doubt, it is. "Goodness" doesn't refer to a superficial, phony, holier-than-thou attitude, nor does it require that a Christian become an old stick-in-the-mud. God doesn't like a phony or a faker, especially a spiritual faker.

So what is goodness, and how do we obtain that level of godly living? Goodness is basically the state of being good, encompassing kindness, generosity, benevolence, and the essence of all things virtuous and excellent. But more than this, goodness includes all those qualities that we see in Jesus Christ—His ambition, His way of making decisions, His manner of overcoming temptations, His ability to love and minister to people, His way of handling frustrations, . . . the list is endless. Goodness is letting the presence and the power of Jesus Christ be absorbed into your mind, thinking about Him and seeking to become and live like He lived.

How do you develop goodness? First, make a conscious, definite choice to become a good person. Determine to pursue goodness and not be halfhearted about it. The reason a lot of people miss the mark is because they are lackadaisical in their efforts. They reserve secret sins in their lives and are unwilling to acknowledge them before God and renounce them. The Bible says that when we hide our sins, God will not give us the power to overcome them. To truly strive for goodness, you must be willing to let God help you overcome all sin in your life. Have you made that choice to become good? Have you honestly let go of that sinful nature, with God's power and help?

Goodness also involves your spiritual capacity in that you must develop a discernment to know the difference between good and evil. You can't always depend on your feelings. We live in a feeling-oriented world. People do something because they "feel like it," or they don't do something because they "don't feel like it." It is important that you develop a value system that is much stronger and much deeper than your emotional state of mind at any given point.

As you develop goodness in your character, *select some role models that you admire.* Of course, the best role model is Christ Himself. Examine the way He lived. But there also are some others whom you admire, others you consider to be genuinely good people. Ask them how God has helped them in their search and progress of spiritual development.

Developing goodness requires you to draw strength from the Holy Spirit. Peter failed the Lord so many times, but when he finally sought God's help, the Holy Spirit gave him courage, spiritual strength, and vitality so that he could become the person of character that God could use. That same help is there for the asking today. Just try it.

The next quality of character development listed in 2 Peter is *knowledge.* This is not the "I'm smarter than you are" or "look what I know" kind of knowledge. Rather, this type of knowledge is character-building knowledge. Peter was an unlearned fisherman, yet he knew the importance of learning and of developing the self-discipline to study. Psalm 119:11 says:

I have laid up thy word in my heart, that I might not sin against thee.

The Word of God is a vital link in the development of knowledge, the knowledge that can help you in your thinking process and understanding process so that you can become the person God wants you to be. A true learner is one who seeks to know the Lord. Are you ambitiously seeking to know the Lord? First John 3:2 tells us:

. . . we shall be like him, for we shall see him as he is.

Christian character is basic Christlikeness. Not only should we seek to know the Lord, but we should seek to know ourselves, often a painful thing to do. As 1 Timothy 4:16 says:

Take heed to yourself and to your teaching; hold to that, for by so doing you will save both yourself and your hearers.

Are you aware of your inner character? Paul said, "Examine yourself." Do you honestly know yourself?

It might help to have a confidential talk with a close friend as you search for an honest, helpful evaluation of yourself. Discover how you are perceived by others. Develop, too, a teachable spirit with the willingness to change your mind and your actions. The older we get, the more difficult it is to change our minds, our patterns of living and acting. But to develop a depth of character, we must be flexible, receptive to constructive criticism from valued friends, and willing and anxious to pursue knowledge as a lifetime adventure.

The third principle or quality mentioned in 2 Peter is *self-control,* or temperance. We all can identify with the apostle Paul's struggle to maintain control. We understand his frustration when he said that the things he knew he shouldn't do were easy to do, yet those things he knew he ought to do were tough to do. Too often, we find ourselves in that same predicament.

Alexander the Great captured the world, yet he could not

rule his own spirit. In a drunken rage, he killed his best friend, and he himself died at age thirty-three. His epitaph read, "He conquered the world. Himself he could not conquer." Many of us are conquering certain areas of our lives—the business world, the social world, and such—but when it comes to conquering ourselves, we fail. Most often, it's not because we lack talent, ability, or the proper contacts, but because we lack character. Self-control is such an important part of God's plan for our lives. It's a plan for us to have a meaningful life, a life of substance and of purpose.

How can you develop self-control? First, choose your environment carefully. Choose the kinds of people with whom you socialize. Proverbs 13:20 says:

> He who walks with wise men becomes wise, but the companion of fools will suffer harm.

Some people will never develop character in their lives because their companions will hinder their growth. Whether in your social life or your business life, don't associate with people who continually pull you down to the point that you do not have the strength to pull away. You will only develop temperance or self-control when you choose the proper environment in which you can thrive.

Next, be willing to counteract bad inclinations with something good. In Romans 12:21 we are told:

> Do not be overcome by evil, but overcome evil with good.

Rather than doing something bad with your life, turn it around and do something good. Sow a thought, reap an action; sow an action, reap a habit; sow a habit, reap a character; sow a character, reap a destiny.

Thirdly, control yourself by making a decision and commitment to rely upon God's power in your life—God's Spirit, not your own. You and I do not have the strength in and of ourselves to conquer our battles. We simply can't do it. That's the reason Jesus Christ sent His Holy Spirit to live inside us, to strengthen us and to help overcome our problems.

A fourth quality in character development is *steadfastness,* or perseverance. You don't just start out. You keep on going until you reach the goal! Abraham Lincoln failed six times in his bid for president of the United States before he was finally inaugurated. The great genius Albert Einstein once said, "I think and think for months, for years—ninety-nine times the conclusion is false; the hundredth time, I'm right!"

Some of you have tried to live for God, and you've failed. Get up and try again! You have tried to overcome bad habits, and you've failed. Try again. Don't just stop. Remain steadfast. Persevere. Character includes that ability to start out on a path and to walk it until you finish. A lot of you have given up too easily. You were progressing beautifully, but you gave up because someone made fun of you or because the effort didn't seem to be worth it. I challenge you, with God's help and power, to get up off that seat of spiritual apathy and indifference and make a personal commitment to follow through, to become the person that God wants you to become.

The quality of *godliness* also is intrinsic to character development. Make your character truly Christlike. Micah 6:8 says that the essence of godliness is to walk humbly with your God. Some people think that to become a great Christian they must become a world-renowned missionary. Of course, this is false. At the same time, don't cheapen the gospel by saying that once you become a Christian it doesn't matter how you live, that God will accept irresponsibility in your Christian life. Salvation is free by God's grace, but godliness is an attitude that permeates every dimension of our lives. It is a willingness to become what God wants us to become. This willingness means that we must recognize and accept God's will in all aspects of our lives on a daily basis. God doesn't just live "over there somewhere," but is present in your home, your business, your social circle, or wherever you go. He is there to help and is aware of everything you do. Feeling the presence of God will help you develop godliness. Become devoted to God. Jesus said, "My will and purpose is to do the will of my Father who sent me." He had a sense of purpose. Godliness involves a willingness to follow God's plan for our lives. Even though it may be tough, God's will is always best, and it always brings about a permanent happiness.

Finally, in your pilgrimage to develop character, nurture others with *brotherly kindness*. This quality is the gregarious, people-loving attitude that continually sees value in others. Brotherly love enables you to have fun relating to other people, to become tender-hearted and affectionate, to like people and enjoy being around them. Will Rogers once said, "I never met a man that I didn't like." This statement doesn't tell us a lot about the people that he met, but it tells us a lot about Will Rogers. What kind of person are you? If you continually find fault with others, you are revealing more about yourself than about those around you. Can you see the good in people? Do you seek to help them in their struggles? Do you share their frustrations and their joys? Brotherly kindness means that we care about others, not withdraw from them. We love them and reach out to them, are willing to forgive them, seek ways to do good for them. Acts 9 tells us of Dorcas, a beautiful woman who made clothes for the poor. She didn't have much herself, but she used what she did have to be kind to others. More of us need to follow her example.

The Bible passage in 2 Peter 5:7 concludes by admonishing us to add *love* to those qualities of character development. This type of love is different than brotherly love. It is *agape* love, or the kind of love that moved God to send His Son to earth to become our Savior—a sacrificial love. The Bible says that to have true character, you must ask God to help you love as He loves. Loving those who can't love you back, who can't do anything nice for you, who can't respond to you—that is true God-like or *agape* love.

Have you ever seen how a farmer prepares the ground to receive seed? He nurtures the soil, fertilizing it and caring for it so that when the seed finally is planted, it becomes productive. Many of us are not productive because our spiritual soil has not been cultivated.

If you have never begun the spiritual pilgrimage to develop sound values and character, I challenge you to allow Jesus Christ to work in and through your life to develop a solid, sincere depth of Christian character.

CONQUERING
ISOLATION

People are lonely
because they build walls
instead of bridges.

– Joseph Fort Newton

9

Hi, how are you?"

It's a standard greeting, said quickly with a smile and slight nod as two acquaintances pass hurriedly along their way. But those words, although usually well-intentioned, ring hollow, void of genuine care about how you *really* are. The words are superficial, said simply to acknowledge another. Any response other than "fine" would be socially unacceptable. In saying it, one is being friendly—but not a friend.

In his collection of *Essays,* Sir Francis Bacon described this societal solitude in a work entitled "On Friendship":

> Little do men perceive what solitude is, and how far it extendeth. For a crowd is not company, and faces are but a gallery of pictures and talk but a tinkling cymbal, where there is no love.

Meaningful friendships are so needed today. We all need friends who care enough to dip beneath the surface, to truly care how we are inside.

Some of you are struggling to develop in-depth, enjoyable,

true relationships with others. You might not have many friends, and you often wonder if anybody really cares about you. Perhaps you have a more inward, introverted personality, and you feel awkward in your attempts to make friends. You watch others with outgoing, delightful, spontaneous personalities as they easily make friends. And you wonder. Can you, too, be fun to be around? How can you develop those deep, lasting friendships?

THE EXAMPLE OF JESUS

The Bible contains many principles that teach us how to get along with one another and how to develop meaningful relationships. God's Word is chock full of examples of great relationships and close friendships. Paul and Timothy in the New Testament and David and Jonathan in the Old Testament are but two examples. There are countless more stories of people who fell in love with God, and then fell in love with one another, developing beautiful friendships that gave them strength and encouragement throughout their lives.

Jesus puts it plainly in John 15:12–17:

This is my commandment, that you love one another as I have loved you. Greater love has no man than this, that a man lay down his life for his friends. You are my friends if you do what I command you. No longer do I call you servants, for the servant does not know what his master is doing; but I have called you friends, for all that I have heard from my Father I have made known to you. You did not choose me, but I chose you and appointed you that you should go and bear fruit and that your fruit should abide; so that whatever you ask the Father in my name, he may give it to you. This I command you, to love one another.

There is no option. Jesus told us to develop friendships with others. For the Christian, there is no way around it. It is a divine commandment from the Lord Himself that we are to love one another.

A man was recently walking through a park when he noticed a lonely, dejected-looking man sitting on a bench. Thinking he might be hungry, the passerby stopped and struck up a conversation. "Sir, do you need some money to buy a meal?" he asked. "No, I don't need any money," the lonely man replied. "What I am hungry for is a good, warm handshake." There comes a time in all of our lives when a good, warm handshake is the most important need we have. We need a smile, someone to pat us on the back and say, "You're looking good," or "You're important to me," or "I believe in you." We need someone to touch our lives in the way that Jesus once touched the lives of others as He walked on this earth. The Bible says He went about doing good. We need more imitators of Christ, more people who care enough to become a friend to someone else. According to Jesus, this is our Christian responsibility.

Although Jesus is our best example, the Bible tells of many other beautiful friendships. In 1 Samuel 18 we find the story of David and Jonathan, who loved each other so much that the Bible says their souls were "knit" together. In Exodus 33:11, the Bible shares the friendship between Moses and God:

> Thus the Lord used to speak to Moses face to face, as a man speaks to his friend.

In James 2:23, Abraham was called "the friend of God." Proverbs 18:24 says:

> There are friends who pretend to be friends, but there is a friend who sticks closer than a brother. That friend is Jesus Christ.

Jesus continually sought the friendship of people who would never be able to do anything great for Him. He was ridiculed and scoffed at for having friends who were prostitutes, tax collectors, those generally scorned by most of the Jewish population. Jesus reached out to all people with an unconditional love. Even as Judas betrayed Him Jesus said, "You are my friend." If only we could pattern our lives after the examples Christ has given us.

A Roman statesman, orator and philosopher named Marcus Cicero once wrote an essay on friendship entitled "De Amicitia" in which he said that a friend is a "second self." In 1841 American author Ralph Waldo Emerson wrote a collection called Essays, which contained a piece entitled "Friendship." In that essay, Emerson called a friend a "masterpiece of nature." He said, "A friend is a person with whom I may be sincere, before whom I may think alone. I would do then with my friends as I do with my books. I would have them where I could find them but would seldom use them." Such friendships are important not only for our spiritual well-being, but also for our psychological well-being.

Sociologists have determined that families which had five or more other families as friends are more likely to be successful families. Additionally, rich friendships which last ten years or more are characteristic of a strong family life and help to guard against family failure.

Many, many individuals have a difficult time trying to name even five friends. A great percentage of people are lonely, including many of you who have few, if any, close friends in which to confide. Be encouraged. Developing meaningful friendships is a sure way to conquer self-imposed isolation and can be one of the greatest adventures of life. You can be assured of God's help if you sincerely want to learn how to make friends.

FRIENDSHIP MEANS . . .

Why is it so difficult to develop these kinds of relationships? One reason is that true friendship requires devotion from both sides. In John 15:14 Jesus said:

You are my friends if you do what I command you.

Friendship means that you are willing to invest your life in another's, and that other person is willing to invest his or her life in your life. It is a mutual commitment. However, many people are afraid of making that commitment because they are afraid of opening themselves up to another person. Taking that step means that they become vulnerable, willing to expose their "real" self, not just the image of what others think they are. That fear becomes a barrier, making it difficult to establish deep friendships.

Also, many individuals don't want to disappoint others, nor do they want others to disappoint them—but that is the risk we run when we open our lives to others. Despite the risks, developing meaningful friendships is worth the effort. It is worth making a commitment to take the initiative, to reach out, and to run the risks inherent in developing lasting relationships.

But how do you make friends? Let's see what the Bible teaches.

Number one: *Be willing to be open with people.* Jesus was quite open and candid with His friends. In John 15:15 Jesus said:

. . . for all that I have heard from my Father I have made known to you.

He was willing to share messages from His Father with His friends, with all the world. He took the risk of disclosing what He had learned. We're usually not that willing to be open with others, particularly those we consider our enemies, for fear that they might use our information against us. We keep information from "subordinates" whom we do not deem worthwhile to reveal ourselves. And we are naturally inclined to not confide in strangers—those we feel would not really appreciate our innermost feelings. But to develop meaningful friendships, we must be willing to be open. We also must learn to graciously accept the openness of our friends, even when they tell us things we might not want to hear. Perhaps you have a bad habit, or a bad attitude, and the friend talks to you about it in love. True friendship allows for such openness.

Number two: *Be willing to take the initiative in developing a friendship.* Don't wait for someone to come to you. Speak up first. Introduce yourself. Invite that new-found friend to lunch, or have him or her over for dinner. In the privacy of a home, people become more relaxed, more willing to let down their guard. You'll find it easy to share in that type of atmosphere. But don't wait for them to reach out to you. Take the initiative.

Number three: *Be willing to give of yourself to another.* In John 15:13 Jesus said:

> Greater love has no man than this, that a man lay down his life for his friends.

The greatest gift you can give to a friend is not a "thing," not something you can buy at the store. The greatest gift is a gift of time, our most precious commodity. Be willing to set aside some of your valuable time to share with others. Such a gift cannot help but strengthen a friendship.

In 1471, two German artists named Hans and Albrecht were struggling to make ends meet while also trying to attend art classes. But they found that their work prevented them from attending classes regularly. One day, Hans decided he should drop out of art class and work extra hard so that Albrecht could attend school full-time. He did, enabling Albrecht to develop into a renowned painter. By the time Hans was able to pursue his art career, his hands were gnarled and disfigured from the hard labor. As a testimony to Hans' love and devotion, Albrecht one day painted a portrait of those calloused hands. Albrecht Durer's painting entitled *Praying Hands* has become world famous as an expression of deep love and appreciation from one friend to another, immortalizing that friendship.

What have you done to extend yourself for another? What efforts have you made to give of yourself for someone else? Ralph Waldo Emerson wrote in his essay "Gifts," "Rings and jewels are not gifts, but apologies for gifts. The only true gift is a portion of thyself." Give love, kindness, joy, understanding, sympathy, tolerance, forgiveness—these are the gifts that build and enrich friendships.

Number four: *Determine to help people like themselves.* A lot of people have a really tough time liking themselves. They seem to be down on themselves all the time. Even when you offer a compliment, they can find a way to twist it around, never fully enjoying your praise. Pledge to find a creative way to change that attitude. Look for opportunities to undergird that person. Lord Chesterfield once told his son, "My son, here is the best way to get people to like you: Make every person like himself a little better, and I promise he will like you very much, indeed." Instead of building yourself up to other people, find ways to build up others. Take time to share a compliment. Proverbs 27:17 says:

> Iron sharpens iron, and one man sharpens another.

God made us so that we can encourage others, so that we can sharpen one another, so that we can build up the image of one another. Let's take advantage of that gift from the Lord!

Number five: *Be natural, not superficial.* One of our greatest temptations in this highly sophisticated society is to put on airs, to try to be somebody or something we are not. Young people today call it the "plastic generation," a phony lifestyle. We need to strive for a naturalness in our demeanor, an unconditional acceptance of others, no matter where they live, what school they attend, what kinds of clothes they wear, what type of car they drive, or what material possessions they own. We need to be aware of how we communicate to others. A slant of the head, slight lift of the eyebrow, or tilt of the nose can say to others, "I don't like you," or "I'm better than you." By becoming aware of our actions and words, we can communicate a message exactly opposite to that. Our smile, our accepting nod, our friendly wink can communicate to others that "I like you," "I enjoy being around you," or "You are important." Strive, too, for naturalness in your dress. As 1 Peter 3:3–4 says:

> Let not yours be the outward adorning with braiding of hair, decoration of gold, and wearing of fine clothing, but let it be

the hidden person of the heart with the imperishable jewel of a gentle and quiet spirit, which in God's sight is very precious.

Number six: *Assume the best about others.* Too many of us are suspicious of others, always trying to figure out how someone is trying to take advantage of us. That's an attitude easily perceived by others, and it will push others away from us every time. Instead, learn to believe in other people. Give them the benefit of the doubt. Develop a tolerant attitude toward them. You cannot develop meaningful friendships if people feel you mistrust them.

Number seven: *Determine not to be overly sensitive.* It's downright childish to wear your heart on your sleeve. Anyone can be offended, if he or she wants to be. I encourage you not to be offended by anything you hear that at first impression appears offensive or abusive. Don't assume the other person is trying to put you down or that they are trying to hurt you. Decide to become a more accepting, tolerant person.

Number eight: *Make all efforts to avoid arguments.* There always will be differences of opinion among people. That diversity of opinion is what makes us all so interesting! Avoid "gun powder" words that, when dropped into a conversation, backfire or explode.

Number nine: *Smile more.* Frowning is hard work. It takes sixty-four facial muscles to form a frown, but only thirteen to form a smile. Too many people are overworking their facial muscles when it's so much easier to "let 'er rip from ear to ear" with a big, friendly smile. Don't proceed through life half mad at the world, just daring someone to smile at you. Turn that around. Wear a smile, and dare someone to show you a frown! As Matthew 7:12 says:

. . . whatever you wish that men would do to you, do so to them. . . .

And number ten: *Be sure that you are working to develop the greatest friendship of all—the friendship of Jesus Christ.*

As you develop that relationship with Him, He will give you the capacity to make friends with others. That's one of the joys of salvation—as you come to know and enjoy God to His fullest, you can better appreciate and love His creations, including other people around you.

It is my prayer that you will not turn away from Jesus, but that you will have the courage and the faith to accept Him as your Savior, your Lord—and your friend.

CONQUERING
DISCOURAGEMENT

The lowest ebb
is the turn of the tide.

— Henry Wadsworth Longfellow

10

One out of every ten people in America today experiences some form of depression and discouragement. So serious is the problem that the ABC television program "20/20" recently devoted an entire special segment to this runaway epidemic. There is hardly a person who does not know depression's signs and symptoms.

When we are discouraged and depressed, we tend to feel as if we are all alone in our problems, that we're the only ones who ever went through the problems we've faced. But the history of discouragement reaches far back to some of the greatest leaders in the Bible. We tend to forget that a leader like King David ever could have been discouraged, as were so many others. After all, David was a man of faith, a man of tremendous talent and dedication. God used him to write many psalms of courage and hope in the Old Testament. His life usually has been held up to us as a pattern of steadfast hope.

Yet David was also a victim of the throes of depression,

and he was forced to endure the direst of circumstances. He was pursued by Saul to the point of death. He was so anxious to escape that he even went to his enemies, the Philistines, seeking refuge. The Philistines said they would provide for him if he would fight in their battles against all other nations except Israel. Naturally, many Philistines were quite suspicious of David and his friends who accompanied him, so eventually the Philistines sent him back from the battlefield to the city of Ziklag and told him to stay there. Alas, David and his company discovered that while they had been away, the Amalekites had raided the city and had destroyed their homes, taking their wives and children captive. David's companions reacted by threatening to stone him to death.

These violent circumstances may seem far removed from our modern experience. But David's depression in the face of the loss of family, friends, and community respect seems very similar to our own. Look at 1 Samuel 30:6:

> And David was greatly distressed; for the people spoke of stoning him, because all the people were bitter in soul, each for his sons and daughters. But David strengthened himself in the LORD his God.

David's sense of abandonment must have been much like our own in many of life's situations today. At the same time, his source of encouragement—"the LORD his God"—is the same source we can draw upon today.

Perhaps the most effective weapon in destroying human lives is this sword of discouragement. An old fable suggests that God and Satan once held a conversation in which God told Satan that he had too much artillery and that He was going to take away every weapon except one. Satan chose to keep the weapon of discouragement, knowing that successful people from all walks of life and of all ages can be affected by it.

Discouragement is indeed a universal experience. It leads people to do and think things they would never even consider under normal circumstances. The tragedy of discouragement is that when we are discouraged, we are unable to reach the full potential God intends for us.

Some people face discouragement in their home lives. Relationships with husbands or wives are not what they ought to be. Others are in dating relationships and are discouraged about the progress, or lack of it, in these situations. Some are discouraged about their children, because they are disappointing to them. Still others are discouraged about school or about personal lives, feeling unable to achieve their goals. They feel low and distraught.

An elderly minister once advised a group of younger ministers, "Young men, remember, whenever you get up to speak, in any situation, on every row, there is always someone with a broken heart." We need to be reminded that the principles of God's Word are sufficient, appropriate, and practical enough to help us deal with any kind of broken heart.

What is discouragement? *Webster's* defines it as the state of being "deprived of courage, hope, or confidence;" or being disheartened. We all know these feelings. We know, too, that it is dangerous to let our moods determine happiness, because the circumstances of life always change.

Discouragement is contagious. When we are discouraged, we affect the people around us—wives, husbands, children, friends. We want to pass discouragement around so we can get other people "down in the dumps" with us. Instead, we must learn to conquer discouragement by dealing with it responsibly—we have too much influence on others surrounding us to simply pass off discouragement as a "blue mood." Perhaps if we could understand the causes of our discouragement, we could deal more effectively with this overwhelming temptation.

IT'S A CRUEL WORLD

The *condition of our world* today sometimes seems enough to cause deep discouragement. We pick up the newspaper and read about neighbors, friends, and innocent victims whose lives have been destroyed by violence. Crime and destruction threaten us and seem to close in on us.

Added to that, the *depersonalization of our society* affects our sense of well-being. We are identified these days by the numbers on our driver's license, credit cards and social security cards. People don't even seem to be interested in who we are—our names or our unique personalities. Even a simple purchase in a store requires that we produce a series of plastic cards that identify us by their long strings of digits. Before long, we begin to feel like just another number in the crowd.

Closer to our inner sense of security, *our work* can often cause discouragement. We live in an achievement-oriented society packed with intense pressure. Ulcers are just one evidence of the high level of stress. The pursuit of success in business can destroy relationships—friends, associates, even families. In pursuing goals, some of us lose those most valuable human relationships which cannot be replaced.

Conditions in our environment—spiritual and physical—also depress us. Weather seems to be insignificant, yet studies indicate we are deeply affected by our surroundings. A number of years ago, a fog in London lingered over the city for four days. The first day, there were a few suicides reported. That number quadrupled on the second day, and then doubled again on the third day. There were more suicides that day than on any other since World War II when German bombers assaulted the city. People simply couldn't cope with their depressing surroundings. On another level, people often live in a spiritual fog. They seem unable to see the meaning and purpose of life. They cannot pierce through to a sense of reality.

Physical exhaustion also leads easily to depression. Our bodies influence our minds and spirits more than we realize. Jesus seemed to know this. In the middle of a busy schedule, He told the disciples to take time to build up physical energy. Jesus often withdrew from the crowds to rest and pray. Today, one of the most spiritual activities in which we can engage is to learn to relax and enjoy leisure activity. Our lives will be extended, as will our witness and our influence in the world. If we don't have time to build up ourselves physically, we will feel the results in our emotions, and discouragement can easily overtake us.

Changing cycles of *human emotion* are a fact of life, and they, too, are an open door to discouragement. Just as seasons change, so do emotions. We "cycle up" emotionally, and then "cycle down" again. It is impossible to live on spiritual and emotional mountaintops all the time. No one in the Bible was ever able to achieve this. Jesus talked about the importance of understanding and dealing with our moods. Because things don't always go our way, that should be no indication that God doesn't love us or isn't interested in our lives.

When we cycle down emotionally, discouragement seems to move in. Pressures and problems in the valleys seem much larger. The point is that we must understand that life is reality, not a fairy tale, and everything is not always going to be super, wonderful, fantastic, or great. Life will bring us times when the going is tough.

At such times, we tend to magnify our own problems. Scientists say the eye of a fly has a magnification system enabling it to see things larger than any human eye can see. Likewise, many people have magnified their problems entirely out of proportion. True, we all have problems. If you were to approach a colleague at work, look him in the eye, and say, "I heard about your problem. I'm really concerned. Is there anything I can do?" Chances are you will get some shocked expressions. Some may ask, "How did you find out about it? Who told you?" We all have problems by virtue of the fact that we are human beings. We mustn't take them and magnify them out of proportion.

Disappointments in life often bring us to the brink of discouragement. These times may come on the job, or from other people who do not live up to our expectations. If a child or friend doesn't act the way we expect them to, or if a situation doesn't turn out the way we planned, we become discouraged.

Perhaps we are expecting too much of others or of ourselves. We want to be better. We want others to be better. But none of us is going to be perfect. That fact doesn't mean we should just give up and say, "Well, I can never be perfect, so I quit."

Oversensitivity to other people's opinions also can send us into discouragement. If we always are looking at the crowd, waiting for compliments and praise, we are doomed to disappointment. Jesus repeatedly spoke of getting our affirmation from Him. As a matter of fact, Jesus said, "Beware when everybody speaks well of you." If everyone you touch thinks you are the greatest person in the world, that probably means you have compromised some area of your life. We don't want to be like the chameleon that crawls up a tree and turns the color of the leaf in order to fit in. There are many people who want to be liked by everybody, but they don't stand for any principles themselves. Being a compromising person, a people-pleaser, can only lead to discouragement.

BEATING THE SYSTEM

How do we handle discouragement? Certainly not by denying our problems or the feelings which they produce. We mustn't say, "I don't hurt," when we really do hurt. In the midst of his discouragement, David didn't say, "I'm going to look in the other direction. All is well." Far from it. The Bible says very honestly, "David was discouraged."

David encouraged himself in the Lord. His example shows how very important it is to admit our problems. Some people try to ignore their discouragement, denying it even exists year after year until the pent-up emotions surface in the form of mental illnesses and emotional turmoil. This very refusal only intensifies the problem. Counselors often ask new clients to retrace their past in order to uncover hidden troubles that had never been dealt with. The greatest lesson we could learn from this professional approach is to stop pretending we have no problems.

Another dangerous trap in avoiding problems is the "one-upmanship" trick. That trick says, "Whatever you have, I have something better," or "I don't care what problem you have—I have a better one. I don't care where you hurt—I hurt in more places than you hurt." That attitude does no one any good.

Some people also take pleasure from seeing how many people they can find to commiserate with them about their condition. Seeking attention in this way never solves any form of discouragement. It only makes us cling to those very problems we need to confront, and it delays any possibility of healing.

The devil knows how susceptible we are to all kinds of discouragement, and he uses the same tricks over and over again to bring us down. But with our faith in Christ and the knowledge that in Him there is nothing we can't handle, we can beat the devil's system!

The first step to conquering discouragement is to make a serious commitment: *I will deal responsibly with myself.* We must stop blaming anyone else or anything else for our own personal weaknesses. So many people love to make excuses. They say, "You don't know my situation. You don't know my job. You don't know what my friend did to me." Or they make the excuse of physical weakness, saying, "I'm getting old. I'm just not the same person I was before. I know I'm quick-tempered, but I just can't handle things the way I used to." Blaming any kind of circumstance for our trouble is dangerous to our mental health.

Instead, we must seek to understand the causes of our discouragement. David should be our example. In the midst of his problem, he asked himself the question, "Why art thou cast down, O my soul?" In Psalm 43:5, we see him stopping to analyze his internal condition to determine why he was troubled.

Recalling great spiritual moments from the past can be a great encouragement when we are feeling troubled. We so easily forget what God has done for us and the good things that have come our way. Think, for instance, how many times you have barely escaped having an automobile accident. You know that if you had been there one split second sooner, the other car would have hit you. When you drove away, you may have said, "God, thank you for sparing my life." He has protected us from hopelessness and disaster so many other times in life. We need to remember those times and not dwell on any adverse circumstances we may be in. When David was discouraged, he practiced the art of remembering. He would say, "This is the same God I knew and loved as a young shepherd boy. I remember the wild animals out there. I remember how God protected me. That same God who protected me back then is going to protect me now in this present serious situation." The God who has seen us through so many circumstances and led us to this point in our lives is going to bring us through again—no matter what!

We can *look to history,* too, to find encouragement. Long ago, barbarians swept down and destroyed the homes and property of many Christians living in Europe. A great man of God named Augustine looked at the situation and realized that God was still powerful. He said, "They lost everything. But have they lost God?" The answer came back from the Christians, "No, we have not lost our God." We, too, may have lost a lot. But have we lost God? No! Even if we have turned our back on Him in despair, He still is there. He still is anxious to help us become the people He wants us to be.

We must *look for the possibilities in the midst of our crisis.* When adversities come, there are still doors open for advancement. Increased knowledge or new opportunities for development probably await us, if only we can see. Booker T. Washington coined a phrase which has encouraged so many today. He spoke of the "advantage of disadvantages." As a young slave, he was not allowed to have an education and he had to carry the books of his white master's son to school every day. About that degrading experience he later said, "I felt like I was a disadvantaged slave boy, but in that process,

I developed an interest in education. That was a disadvantage which became my advantage." Later, Washington became a great leader and an encouragement to many other disadvantaged people. Like him, we have things in our lives which seem to be severe disadvantages. But they might in some way be the doorway to later advantages.

Some of the best things can happen to us in the worst of circumstances. Ralph Waldo Emerson once said, "While man sits on the cushion of advantages, he goes to sleep. When he is pushed, tormented and defeated, he has a chance to learn something." We need to remember that some of the best things that can happen to us frequently come out of the worst possible situations.

When we have trouble, we need to *bring our plight into the presence of God.* When David was discouraged, he quickly got alone with God. In the same way, we need to pray: *Lord, I have a tremendous problem, and I know You are a great God. You have the ability to help me overcome it. I need Your help and strength.* Psalms 16:8 says:

> I keep the LORD always before me; because he is at my right hand, I shall not be moved.

Even in the face of death, we can be confident in God. Some time ago, a couple sang a duet entitled "God Will Take Care of You" at a Sunday morning worship service. The next week, the wife went into the hospital for serious lung surgery. She said to her husband, "Let's not forget the song we sang last week together at church. 'Be not dismayed, what e're betide. God will take care of you.' " [1] The couple claimed that beautiful song as their testimony, and through all of that difficulty, they felt the strength that only God can give.

When we are discouraged for any reason, we can *fill our thoughts with spiritual affirmations.* We need the Bible above everything else. When we pick it up and begin to read, we find ourselves thinking the kinds of thoughts God wants us to have. Meditation on the Bible always has that effect upon us. That's why we call it God's Word.

We read, "This is the day the Lord has made. I will rejoice and be glad in it." And then we read, "Praise God from whom all blessings flow," or "Be of good cheer. I have overcome the world" or "I can do all things through Christ who strengthens me." Over and over again we find these positive words supplying us with confidence, hope, help, and strength for our daily thinking.

Discouragement can be preparation for renewal. If anyone is in a discouraging situation right now, God may be saying, "Now, I want to do something special in your life. Let this not be a discouragement for you. Let it be an open door through which you can learn from Me." Lewis Mumford, an American social philosopher, once said, "In time of trouble is the time to prepare for the renewal of life."

English poet John Milton's great work *Paradise Lost* was written in the midst of the chaos of England's civil war. John Bunyan, the famous English writer and preacher, wrote the great Christian parable *Pilgrim's Progress* while in Bedford Prison, where he unjustly was held. Rather than give in to discouragement, Bunyan used the inspiration of God to write this great work of faith and courage. These men knew what we, too, can know in a very personal way. There is a mountain behind every valley, and God will provide the way to it. He will lead us up to a level place, and then on to His highest goals for our lives.

If we truly want to overcome discouragement, we can *look beyond ourselves rather than remaining caught within ourselves.* We must learn to be helpful to others. We often remain discouraged because we are selfish. We want someone to do something for us. But when we turn around and begin to take an interest in other people, discouragement seems to melt away. We are not thinking about how we are feeling, but are concentrating on our neighbor.

Expanding our personal faith is another key to overcoming

discouragement. Prominent psychologist William James once said, "Every sort of energy and endurance of courage and capacity for handling life's evil is set free in those who have religious faith." [2]

I am convinced that only with Jesus Christ in our lives do we have that personal faith and solid forgiveness which assures us of the confidence of God's eternal presence. With God, we have the capacity to face the demands of life. The solution to every discouraging problem can become ours as we daily search the Scriptures and pray to understand the application of God's words to our hearts and lives.

God has provided us with the ultimate resource to overcome every possible form of discouragement. May we enter in more fully to that ultimate resource. We must determine to walk forward with Jesus Christ.

CONQUERING
LONELINESS

The body is a house of many windows:
there we all sit, showing ourselves
and crying on the passers-by
to come and love us.

> – Robert Louis Stevenson
> *Virginibus Puerisque*

11

Loneliness is the top emotional problem facing society today. Without a doubt, everyone is touched by it, affected by it, often emotionally wrecked by it. The key to emotional health and vigor often lies in knowing how to overcome or conquer loneliness.

Not long ago, a prominent doctor was asked what he believed to be the most serious and most devastating disease facing people today. His reply? "Loneliness." Despite crowds of people who surround us and despite numerous acquaintances in the workplace, neighborhoods, churches, and schools, people still feel lonely. The "disease" touches all of us at some point in our lives, and doctors, alone, have been unable to offer a cure.

One of the most popular songs of the 1960s—sung by the Beatles, one of the most popular rock groups of that day—carried a verse that was repeated over and over and over again. "Hey, look at all those lonely people. Hey, look at all those lonely people. . . ." [1] Apparently the rock stars, too, had seen the sad, telltale expressions of loneliness on the faces of count-less people in every city, town, and village they visited. The loneliness and estrangement is so deep-seated that it has be-come etched in the faces of millions of people at all levels of society today. It's not hard to see. Just scan the faces of the crowd the next time you are in a football stadium or are walking along a busy downtown street in a metropolitan city.

Jesus knew what it was like to be alone. There were many moments of His life when the Bible tells us that He slipped away into seclusion. But He was alone—never lonely. Through God's Word, we can find hope and help for dealing with the difficulty of loneliness. In John 16:31–33, Jesus offers assur-ances for the lonely:

> Do ye now believe? Behold, the hour cometh, yea, is now come, that ye shall be scattered, every man to his own, and shall leave me alone: and yet I am not alone, because the Father is with me. These things I have spoken unto you, that in me ye might have peace. In the world ye shall have tribulation: but be of good cheer; I have overcome the world (KJV).

In Psalm 46, David provides further comfort to the lonely:

> God is our refuge and strength, a very present help in trouble. Therefore will not we fear, though the earth be removed, and though the mountains be carried into the midst of the sea; Though the waters thereof roar and be troubled, though the mountains shake with the swelling thereof. Selah. There is a river, the streams whereof shall make glad the city of God (vv. 1–4, KJV).

"I NEED SOMEBODY TO TALK TO"

Since loneliness is such a universal problem, you might be one of those feeling lonely today. You might be one of the most active adult members of your church or community, yet you still feel lonely. You might be one of those back-slapping, hand-shaking extroverts—always smiling, laughing, joking, and enjoying the limelight in a crowd. Yet, deep down inside, you might ache with loneliness. That smile, laugh, or joke might help cover up the hurt and pain of loneliness, but it doesn't make it go away.

Perhaps you are a teenager who feels that nobody really loves you, that nobody really cares. Maybe you have been rejected by your peers. Perhaps you have had difficulty in finding dates. You might find that you don't "fit in" with the popular crowd at school. You don't have the "right" personality or can't afford to dress in the designer-label clothes that you see other teenagers wear.

You might be a child living with only one parent and are feeling the frustration, estrangement, and loneliness that go along with living in a broken home. If so, you have lots of company. One of every five children in America today lives in a one-parent home.

I was in my church office one Sunday afternoon when I heard a knock at the door. I opened it to find a mother and her seven-year-old daughter. They had nowhere to go and wondered if the church could help them. My wife and I took them into our home for about two weeks, trying to offer consolation and support. We discovered that the woman had married her husband in Germany while he was stationed there in the service. They since had returned to the United States, but their marital life had deteriorated to the point that he had threatened her life. Terrified and without a job, she took her daughter and fled, often sleeping with the little girl in the back seat of her car.

The mother was able to find a job in another part of the city, and shortly, they moved out of our home into their own place. Yet, for several weeks we got telephone calls—sometimes in the middle of the night—from the little girl. Her mother often would have to work late into the night or even until the wee hours of the morning, leaving the frightened little girl by herself. "I'm all alone and I need somebody to talk to," she would tell us between the tears. That scene remains a vivid picture in my mind today of the loneliness that so many children face.

SURROUNDED BY STRANGERS

Maybe you are one of the millions of adults going through your own middle-age crisis with all of its pressures, problems, and temptations. You might not feel at peace with yourself and are finding that people or material items that would normally not be attractive to you are suddenly sources of temptation. You feel helpless in the face of all the pressures, alone in your thoughts, and lonely on your life's journey.

Perhaps you are one of the ever-increasing numbers of elderly citizens in this nation, and you are experiencing a loneliness like you've never felt before. You feel pushed aside, unwanted, unloved. Whether you live in a retirement home, in your own home, or with relatives, you can't shake the feeling of being rejected, alone, and lonely. Not long ago, an elderly person told me, "I'm really not afraid of dying, but I *am* afraid of living until I die. I don't like the daily monotonous routine of being over in the corner by myself." How sad! So many people, though they may be seventy-five to ninety-five years old, have sharp, keen minds. They may not have the ability to maneuver like they once did, but they would rather cope with immobility or decreased activity than with the hurt and agony of being lonely.

You might be one of the millions of single adults who find themselves alone, whether it's because they never married, are divorced, or lost a spouse through death. In Dallas, Texas, 52 percent of the population are single. Many of these singles live by themselves. They face all of the frustrations, temptations, and pressures that go along with being alone. And, even though there are hundreds of thousands of others in the city, these people are surrounded by strangers.

There have been many times that I, too, have felt alone. My first recollection of feeling alone and abandoned was when

I was enrolled in kindergarten in Fort Worth, Texas, where my parents attended seminary. I'll never forget being left at school that first day. All of the other children—and adults— were strangers. I remember running to the big fence that sur- rounded the kindergarten grounds. I clutched the chainlink fence, sobbing as I watched my mother drive away. I felt de- serted and very much alone. There have been many times since that dreadful day that I have felt very lonely.

Sadly, we often find that we do things when we are lonely that we normally would not do otherwise. Businessmen, profes- sional women, teenagers, homemakers, even children will all act in ways that they usually do not act, simply because they are lonely. As teenagers or adults, we might find ourselves being tempted to have illicit relationships to cover up our loneli- ness. As children, we might find ways to draw attention—and love—to ourselves, even if it means behaving badly.

No matter what your age, or no matter what your reason for feeling lonely or alone, there is hope—there *is* a cure! Through God's Word, we can find strength and support, peace and an ever-abiding presence.

ALL MIRRORS AND NO WINDOWS

To understand how to deal with loneliness, let's first look at exactly what we mean when we talk about loneliness.

There are several basic types of loneliness—a loneliness that we create for ourselves; loneliness created by circumstances beyond our control; spiritual loneliness; psychological loneli- ness; and loneliness created by the modern society in which we live.

When we react adversely to others, or find ourselves criticiz- ing other people and constantly putting them down, it's not hard to guess what will happen next. Those people are going to back away from us. They'll not want to associate with us and often will go out of their way to avoid us. We'll wonder why we don't have many friends. It's because we've created loneliness for ourselves through our negative actions and attitudes.

Other times, we might feel alone and lonely due to circumstances beyond our control, particularly through the death of a loved one. Perhaps you've lost a husband or wife, or have experienced the loss of a relative or friend. You are angry with God for having taken that loved one from you. You feel abandoned and alone. You can't do anything about it, and now you are left all alone.

You may feel as though you are spiritually dead, far, far removed from God. You don't have that real purpose, happiness, and sense of meaning in life that come about only through a relationship with God through Jesus Christ. You are spiritually hungry, spiritually dead, and spiritually lonely.

You might also feel isolated psychologically from others, even if you find yourself in the midst of a crowd of people. You might be sitting in a room with hundreds, perhaps thousands, of other people, yet feel absolutely alone, without companions or friends.

Loneliness is a life that is all mirrors and no windows. Lonely people seem to have a knack for looking inward instead of outward. It's so easy to ask, "What can other people do for *me?* What can the church provide for *me?* What can the community offer to *me?* What can my friends contribute to *me?*" We often do not ask what we can do for others, especially to help alleviate *their* loneliness.

I am convinced that loneliness is mostly self-pity. A victim tends to shut himself in and others out, and everybody avoids him because nobody loves a self-pitier. And the sorrier he feels for himself, the lonelier he becomes. He spins his own cocoon.

Often, we find that our modern society has led us to this point of loneliness. We strive for individuality and are reduced to anonymity, a mere number on someone else's computer list. Names no longer matter. I could take out my wallet right now and hold up several cards with my name imprinted on them. But it's not my name that identifies me on these cards—

it's the numbers that are important. Think about it—driver's license numbers, Social Security numbers, credit card numbers, insurance numbers, license plate numbers, street address numbers, phone numbers, checking and savings account numbers—the list goes on and on and on. We become numbers, and if we're not careful, we find ourselves "numbered" in so many relationships of life that we begin to think of ourselves as just a number, rather than a live, caring human being who can laugh and cry and feel emotions, and who can care deeply and needs to be cared for.

Perhaps we can begin to avoid these types of loneliness if we can understand a bit more about what causes loneliness.

IT'S LONELY AT THE TOP

It's often just this simple: most people don't like to be alone. We frequently find it difficult, if not almost impossible, to cope with being by ourselves. One friend recently told me, "I am fed up with inventing devices for getting through twenty-four hours a day. I'm tired of it. I don't like to be by myself, and I've been making up things to do."

Letting ourselves become consumed with an abnormal need to be loved also can lead to loneliness. I've noticed this many times, particularly with parents trying to let go of their sons or daughters. "Giving up" a child who gets married or goes off to college is hard to do, and not being able to let go often will aggravate those feelings of loneliness.

One mother had a phone installed in her daughter's college dormitory room so that she could call her several times a day. Naturally, the daughter felt pressured by her mother. She felt her mother didn't trust her and constantly was checking up on her. After a while, the daughter became so annoyed by her mother's persistence that she refused to answer the phone and left instructions for her roommate to tell her mother she wasn't there, even if she was. What was happening was that the mother was experiencing being left very much alone. She had an abnormal need to be loved by her daughter, and it left her uncomfortable and angry when she couldn't talk with her daughter several times a day. While this situation may not be entirely typical, it is probably not far from everyday occurances as many parents struggle with the fear of loneliness when their children grow up and leave home.

The absence of friends and intimate relationships in life also leads to loneliness. Without close friends and intimate, loving relationships, we feel as if we are missing out on something everybody else has. For this reason, the church can be vitally important in providing opportunities for people to develop mutual friendships and meaningful relationships with others. Those without meaningful relationships outside of the business community find themselves much more susceptible to loneliness. So often in the business world, friendships are based on what each person can provide for the other financially or in terms of professional advancement. Once you "arrive" at the top of the professional or career ladder, you usually find loneliness there, too. It's the loneliness of success, of finally making it to the top. Now, because of your higher status or position, you find that the friends and associates you once felt close to no longer feel that sense of camaraderie or kinship with you. Those kinds of business or professional relationships often are transitory and temporary—not the lasting, loving relationships and friendships that can be nurtured in the church or home. If business friends are your only friends, you probably will find it more difficult to overcome the problems associated with loneliness.

Superficial success in the business world coupled with subtle and not-so-subtle societal pressures to collect material possessions can be the root of perhaps the most serious kind of loneliness possible—spiritual loneliness. Despite all the materialism and all of the so-called "success" that surrounds average Americans who live in an affluent community, I remain convinced that they are struggling with a deep spiritual loneliness. Many of the problems in our communities today are there because people are unable to deal with the spiritual loneliness inside.

What can be done to wipe out spiritual loneliness, or any other type of loneliness?

CURES FOR LONELINESS

One of the first steps to take in curing loneliness is to recognize that loneliness is a problem in your life that needs conquering. Conquering loneliness begins with a personal one-on-one encounter within your life. If there has never been a time when you prayed: *Yes, Lord Jesus, I am lonely and I need You. I want You. I acknowledge sin in my life and want to turn my life over to You. I accept You as Savior and Lord in my life—* then it must begin here.

Martin Mueller was a minister in Germany who was imprisoned by the Nazis for four years because of his faith. He recalled feeling overwhelming loneliness, but told of never being alone. He felt spiritual contact with God and with other believers because of his deep abiding faith in the Lord.

He had already discovered what you can discover today— that Jesus Christ is a friend who is truly understanding, sympathetic, and invigorating. He sees you more closely and clearly than you can see yourself. He can bring you out of your shell and help you overcome loneliness. Indeed, He is that friend of Proverbs 18:24 that "sticketh closer than a brother."

Jesus becomes that close friend when you accept Him as your Savior. As Hebrews 13:5–6 tells us:

> Let your conversation be without covetousness; and be content with such things as ye have: for he hath said, I will never leave thee, nor forsake thee. So that we may boldly say, The Lord is my helper, and I will not fear what man shall do unto me (KJV).

To avoid loneliness, we should *experience the presence of Christ daily.* What does this mean? It doesn't mean to practice the "holiday commitment"—that Easter/Christmas syndrome that tempts us to be "super spiritual" or "extra religious" only around holiday times. Jesus Christ is ever present, always near, not just available at Christmas or Easter. I encourage you to become aware and sensitive to the presence of Christ in your life on a daily basis. Wake up in the morning with a song. You don't have to be a Sandi Patti or a Pat Boone to sing praises to God. And there's just something about singing that automatically lifts the heart and spirit.

One friend told me that before going to bed each night, she would visualize Jesus Christ sitting in a chair beside her bed with a smile on His face. She shared how that visual image helped her to pray and to go to sleep without a cloud of loneliness hovering about. She said, "You know, I try to live with the consciousness that Jesus is all around me."

God's love doesn't come and go. It's not a temporary love. Jeremiah 31:3 teaches:

> I have loved you with everlasting love; therefore, I have continued my faithfulness to you.

Isaiah 54:10 shows us:

> For the mountains may depart and the hills be removed, but my steadfast love shall not depart from you.

In addition to experiencing the presence of Christ daily, try to *focus your attention and energy on other people* rather than centering your concerns on yourself. One doctor told a patient recently, "Your trouble, ma'am, is nothing but aggravated selfishness. You ought to get involved with others and volunteer to do something for someone else." I wonder how many of us could take that prescription today? We're often plagued with loneliness simply because we sit around with nothing to do. We wonder why no one ever asks us to do anything, but we don't think to volunteer. There are so many needs to be met in our world today, and there are people just begging to be recognized, loved, and cared for. Taking the time to visit someone who is hurting or aching with loneliness not only will be meaningful to them, but it especially will be fulfilling to you.

Try calling your church to ask, "What members of the church are hospitalized? I have a few hours. I thought I'd go down to the hospital and visit a few people. If there is someone in the church who needs a visit, I'd like to go see them." Or volunteer to spend a spare afternoon, weekday, or weekend helping out at your church, community center, or neighborhood charitable organization. You'll be surprised how receptive the staff members will be to your willingness to share your time and energy.

Perhaps some of you have friends with small children. Volunteer to baby-sit for an evening to allow the parents a night out by themselves, or take the children to a zoo or park one Saturday afternoon to allow the parents some free time alone.

The point is, you will not overcome loneliness as long as your thinking centers around what other people can do for you. Reach out to other people and show them what *you* can do for *them*.

Then, *learn to practice "present enjoyment."* The apostle Paul said, "I have learned in whatsoever state I am to be content." This attitude is extremely important in curing loneliness. Don't base your happiness on what is going to happen tomorrow, or next week, or next year. There are some people who plan trips every couple of months. They never really enjoy the trip they are on because they're too busy thinking about the next one. Consequently, they never enjoy what they have. Their happiness is always down the road somewhere. You will not be able to overcome loneliness if you cannot learn to enjoy today—the present—to its fullest.

Another "cure" for loneliness is to *become active in your church in a meaningful way.* The potential for service is one of the great things about the body of Christ in the local church. The church should be a place of involvement, participation, and service, not just a place where you go to listen to a Sunday sermon. Serving in the church will help to overcome feelings of loneliness and insignificance in life. The church is a place where you can develop skills and become involved in an unselfish way in the lives of others.

And finally, *look for creative possibilities in your loneliness.* If you live alone, recognize that sometimes you may *need* to be alone. Great American philosopher Henry David Thoreau once said, "I went to the woods because I wished to live deliberately; to front only the essential facts of life; and to see if I could not learn what it had to teach and not when I came to die discover that I had not lived."

Maybe you need to ask God to help you interpret or better understand your life and why you have been placed in a situation of being alone. Then, through understanding the circumstances, you will be able to make a greater contribution to the world.

A great missionary, David Livingstone, once told students at the University of Glasgow about his sixteen years alone in Africa, serving the Lord. "Shall I tell you what it was that sustained me in my exiled years?" Livingstone asked the students. "It was the Word of Christ. It was the promise he made when he said, 'Lo, I am with you always.' "

To those of you who right now feel lonely, take those precious and priceless words of consolation and assurance from the Lord:

"Lo, I am with you always."

CONCLUSION

How are you responding to life's challenges? Christianity is not just one possible option to enable us to handle the difficult issues of life—it is the only meaningful and fulfilling way! Jesus not only provides an understanding regarding what the problems in life are but He also provides a way of solving these problems. He dwells in us as believers to give us wisdom and power. And through Him, we can become winners in even the most difficult situations of life.

The difference in mediocrity and greatness in life is determined by what we do with our high and holy impressions! God gives us truth based on our willingness to obey it. But the "truth will set you free" only if you choose to hear it and put in into practice.

Remember that *life is personal* for all of us—no one can make our decisions for us. We appreciate our friends, but major decisions can only be made within ourselves. *Life is a process.* Each day we are becoming more of what we think, believe, feel, and practice. Pressures and problems are real for all of us, and it is so important that we are growing in our ability and maturity to respond to situations that can strengthen us or weaken us. *Life forces decision.* You make your own choices, whether you say "I will decide to do this . . ." or "I will not do this . . ." or "I'll think about it." Any of these attitudes represent a decision that you make about your life and future.

Let me encourage you to begin with just a few of these

chapters at first and put their suggestions into practice. As you gain strength and victory, you then should move on to another chapter. We must not get discouraged when we are unable to achieve complete accomplishment in each area. It takes time, but there must be a beginning.

On one occasion, I was faced with a challenging opportunity to begin a building program that would cost over eight million dollars. It seemed so big and impossible from our new congregation. Mary Kay, the founder and chairman of the board of Mary Kay Cosmetics, took my hand, looked into my eyes, and with a spark of confidence and assurance said, *"You can do it!"* That supercharged me, motivated me, and energized me.

May I say to you now, *"You can do it, too!"* You can overcome every problem, solve every difficulty, make progress in every area of your life—if you will begin now. Ask God to dwell in you with His power, to restore you to a right relationship with Him. You can do this by inviting Christ into your life—your will—your "decision-making room." I am confident that beautiful changes will begin to occur in you that will greatly affect not only your life, but also the lives of everyone you meet. The choice you make *will* have an impact on this life— as well as the life to come in eternity. What will you decide?

NOTES

Chapter 2
1. S. I. McMillen, *None of These Diseases* (Old Tappan, NJ: Fleming H. Revell, 1963), 71.
2. Ibid., 72.

Chapter 3
1. E. Stanley Jones, *Mastery* (Nashville: Abingdon Press, 1955), 229.
2. As quoted by Rev. Bruce Wideman, Warrington Presbyterian Church, 9 June 1974.
3. Jones, *Mastery,* 231.

Chapter 4
1. Virginia Brasier, "Time of the Mad Atom." Quoted by Norman Vincent Peale, "How to Cool It and Relax," *Creative Help for Daily Living* (Pauling, NY: Foundation for Christian Living, 1971).
2. Arnold Toynbee, *A Study of History* (Oxford University Press, 1954).
3. Dr. Herbert Vincent, "A Simple, Cost-Free, and Comfortable Way to Combat Job Tension," *Nation's Business* Magazine Dec 1976, 64:29.
4. William M. Elliot, Jr., *For the Living of These Days* (Richmond, VT: John Knox Press, 1946), 122.
5. C. T. Winchester, *The Life of John Wesley* (New York: The Macmillan Co., 1906), 117, 119.
6. Psalm 23, translated by Toki Miyashina from the *Japanese Bible.*
7. Harold Blake Walker, *The Power to Manage Yourself* (New York: Harper & Bros. Publ., 1955), 86.

Chapter 5
1. James Dobson, *Hide and Seek* (Old Tappan, NJ: Fleming H. Revell, 1974).
2. Dick Dickinson, "Because God Loves Me." Used by permission.

Chapter 6
1. "Don't Fence Me In," words and music by Cole Porter. © 1944 by Harms, Inc.
2. Ray Stannard Baker, *American Chronicle* (New York: Charles Scribner's Sons, 1945), 181.

Chapter 7
1. William Danforth, *I Dare You* (St. Louis, MO: I Dare You Co., 1976).

Chapter 10
1. Civilla D. Martin, W. Stillman Martin, "God Will Take Care of You." © 1905.
2. Quoted by Kenneth Hildebrand, *Achieving Real Happiness* (New York: Harper Bros., Publ., 1955), 146.

Chapter 11
1. "Lonely People," words and music by Dan & Katherine Peck, © 1974 by W. B. Music Corp. The Artist: America.